DIPLOMACY
AND THE
AMERICAN
DEMOCRACY

David D. Newsom

DIPLOMACY
AND THE
AMERICAN
DEMOCRACY

Indiana University Press

Bloomington and Indianapolis

Manufactured in the United States of America

Library of Congress Cataloging-in-Publication Data
Newsom, David D.
  Diplomacy and the American democracy.

  Includes index.
  1. United States—Foreign relations administration.
2. United States—Diplomatic and consular service.
I. Title.
JX1706.N535   1988   353.0089   87-45438
ISBN 0-253-31816-5
ISBN 0-253-20470-4 (pbk.)

92 91 90 89 88 1 2 3 4 5

O wad some Pow'r the giftie gie us
To see oursels as others see us!
It wad frae mony a blunder free us,
And foolish notion . . .

ROBERT BURNS

CONTENTS

Preface

This book is an effort by an American diplomatic practitioner to examine how the United States conducts its affairs with other nations. It attempts to address, if, perhaps, not fully to answer, why the United States is not as successful in the extension of its influence and the promotion of its objectives as many of its citizens believe it should be.

In forty years as a participant and observer of American diplomacy, I have encountered strikingly contrasting questions at home and abroad. Americans have asked me why so many people in the world are anti-American, given our generosity and our demonstrated desire for peace and freedom; why the Soviet Union seems to have greater success than we do in many regions; and why we seem so often to be taken by surprise by events that affect our interests. Foreigners ask me why Americans pay so little attention to what others think; why Americans are so preoccupied with the Soviet Union; and why the United States seems so often to involve itself where no discernible U.S. interests are present.

The two sets of questions suggest a contradiction that may help explain some of America's problems and frustrations. The Americans' view of themselves and their assumptions about how the rest of the world regards the United States are different in important respects from the way other nations actually view America. Many observers suggest that problems in U.S. relations with other countries stem from faulty intelligence, disorganized decision making, or ineffective diplomacy. These may be fair criticisms, but underlying such problems are uniquely American attitudes and expectations toward other nations. Much of what the United States does abroad is designed to satisfy national impulses that grow out of how Americans view the world. Programs and policy initiatives are frequently undertaken that are based more on illusions than on knowledge.

To understand the difficulties the United States faces in its foreign relations, a look at traditional diplomatic activity is not enough. The problems and the strengths of the American democracy in intercourse with others can be understood not only in terms of attitudes, but in the broader context of the many elements of the executive branch involved in foreign affairs, the Congress, the media, and the private sector groups that seek to influence the process. How other nations see the United States, how they judge its intentions, and how they react to its efforts are determined by the total projection of the American society and government abroad through these many channels, both official and private.

This is being written during the administration of Ronald Reagan. The Reagan administration has highlighted many of the attitudes toward foreign relations deeply held in American society. As the history of this period has demonstrated, however, the strong desire for an assertion of U.S. strength, largely in military terms, is countered by the efforts of a large number of Americans to find less aggressive ways of exercising the nation's influence. This constant debate between assertive nationalists and more cautious internationalists has gone on in every recent administration. Generalizations are, therefore, subject to many qualifications. Nevertheless, as this is written, the more assertive trends seem paramount; many of the difficulties and contradictions I seek to address stem from these trends.

To speak of American attitudes and practices is, of course, broadly to generalize about a vast and varied people. I presume to do so not on the basis of any profound or systematic survey, but because I have encountered so often the views I am describing in my official experiences as well as in numerous sessions in the United States and abroad in organizations, on campuses, and with general audiences. I acknowledge, also, a heavy emphasis on experiences in the newly independent nations. In so doing, I am influenced not only by the many years I spent as a U.S. diplomat in these countries, but also by a recognition of how much the focus of American frustration in the postwar years has been toward this so-called Third World. I am bolstered in my confidence in the conclusions of this book by the observations of many others, some of whom I quote. I fully acknowledge, however, that there are many in the United States who may not agree and to whom these generalizations do not apply.

My comments are not intended to be critical, but to help us see ourselves as many others see us. To do so is not to detract from the greatness of our country or from its unique contributions to the world. The purpose is more to explain from the vantage point of someone who, it is hoped, has seen from both sides some of the aspects of our relations with others that trouble ourselves, our friends, and our adversaries.

The gestation of the book began in 1981, at the initiative of the publisher, John Gallman, shortly after my retirement from the United States Foreign Service. Its premises have been further bolstered by a semester spent on a Fulbright grant in the United Kingdom in 1986. Although the book has been many years in the making, the events of these years seem only to confirm that serious differences exist between America's understanding of the rest of the world and foreign perceptions of America.

In the preparation of this book, I am indebted to John Gallman for his encouragement and to my wife, Jean, for her constant support, her observations on our experiences, and her sensitive editing of the final draft.

DIPLOMACY
AND THE
AMERICAN
DEMOCRACY

I

𝒟

A CHANGING DIPLOMACY

IN THE DIPLOMATIC LIFE of the late 1940s, the traditional diplomat of the 1930s could still feel at home. Although the world had been convulsed by war, diplomatic life largely followed prewar conventions. Travel was mainly by ship. People "dressed for dinner" wherever possible. Formal dress was worn on state occasions. Women wore hats and gloves to pay formal calls, and cards were still exchanged. Diplomatic communications were drafted in the polite phrases of the nineteenth century. While the telegram was used, much of the business was transacted in despatches that were addressed personally to the Secretary of State or Foreign Minister and ended with the traditional "Your Obedient Servant." Most messages went via diplomatic "bags" carried by couriers. Diplomatic immunity was scrupulously observed. Empires still existed. The world was Europe-centered. Personal meetings of kings and presidents were considered rare and special events. Senior officials stayed largely at home and let their envoys conduct business with other nations. Widely accepted rules of diplomacy were generally followed. Diplomats did not delve openly below the surface of another country. They dealt largely, if not exclusively, with the foreign ministry.

Suddenly these styles and conventions began to change—and change rapidly. Diplomacy became less formal and more pressured. The airplane became the mode of diplomatic travel. The jet age made possible, as never before in history, meetings among national leaders. The speed and availability of transportation facilitated the vastly increased number of international meetings. Once a nation had been represented at such a meeting by its foreign minister, it proved difficult to reduce the level of representation at subsequent meetings. Diplomacy thus moved up to personal contacts among ministers. The role of ambassadors and traditional diplomats was, in many areas, reduced to that of briefer and travel agent. The pace of diplomacy had also been quickened by the seriousness and urgency of events; the telegram and the telephone became major instruments of diplomatic communication between ambassadors and their capitals and even to a growing extent between cabinet level officials and heads of state. The speed of events and diplomacy required more rapid answers; there was less time to think.

The more advanced nations created diplomatic communications networks that depended less on couriers and laborious cryptographic methods and more on automatic computerized means of transmission that were faster and more secure. The same technology also gave the information media the advantage of speed. Satellites and television could bring not only news but views of major events to audiences well ahead of the labored and considered messages of the diplomats. In the democracies, foreign affairs became increasingly more open and more under the pressure of domestic concerns. Political leaders, responding to the demands of publics and parliaments, at times spoke and acted before the assessments of their own diplomats had arrived.

Rapid communications meant also that the diplomat was on a shorter leash. Except in those rare instances when a diplomat was beyond the reach of rapid communications, negotiations were often managed by telephone from the foreign office and augmented by flying visits from home-based officials. The politician became diplomat and, in many cases, changed the context of diplomacy.

The proliferation of higher level contacts meant, also, that the offices attached to heads of governments dealt with counterparts abroad on issues believed to be too sensitive for the traditional foreign ministries. The Elysee in Paris, the Prime Minister's office in London, the Bundeskanzlei in Bonn, and the National Security Council staff in Washington constituted a new network for the conduct of the most important diplomatic business.

Diplomacy at the higher level had serious disadvantages. Political leaders and their followers were compelled to show achievement—or the appearance of achievement. The time for discussions, particularly if interpreters were required, was brief. The close proximity of the press and the pressure for "stories" meant that the focus was often more on the public aspect than on the diplomatic.

While technology altered the pace and style of diplomacy in many ways, two major political developments in the postwar period did more than any technology to change the style and scope of international relations: the process of decolonization and the confrontation between the Soviet Union and the Western powers.

With the breakup of European empires, more than a hundred new nations became independent. In the greatest political revolution in history, more than one-half of the peoples of the world saw old flags hauled down and new ones raised. A United Nations was created that was soon dominated by the new nations. The two greatest powers felt deterred by the nuclear threat; nevertheless, lesser conflicts arose as the colonial mantle was removed from areas of traditional unrest. The agendas of diplomacy were expanded to include highly technical subjects related to economic development, arms control, the environment, the transfer of technology, and the challenges to sovereignty and privacy of the computer. Trade became a central issue, for both developed and developing countries.

The process of decolonization ran parallel with the increased postwar activity of the Soviet Union. The Soviet Union's incorporation of Eastern European nations into a tightly controlled zone of influence became a dominant and frustrating issue in the diplomacy of Western nations. East-West issues produced an endless series of negotiations. The Soviets seemed to see negotiations not as a means to resolve problems, but as a way to advance political goals. Efforts around tables to deal with arms control and a host of related issues lasted years; diplomacy became an endurance contest. The Soviet Union perpetuated a confrontational style of diplomacy supported by clandestine involvement in the internal affairs of nations and an active worldwide propaganda program.

The end of World War II found the United States at center stage in this changed world, the most powerful nation in the world. Neither its citizens nor its diplomats were fully prepared for the profound growth in the nation's responsibilities. Nevertheless, dramatic diplomatic achievements such as the Austrian Treaty, the Trieste settlement, and the treaty with Japan were possible, benefitting from a national consensus and a well defined objective, the reconstruction of the postwar world.

I was treated once to a dramatic example of America's contribution to that reconstruction. While waiting in the anteroom of Chancellor Kreisky of Austria a few years ago, I was joined by one of the Chancellor's aides. After apologizing for a slight delay in the appointment, he said, "But while we are waiting I would like to show you something of importance to both of us." He led me to a painting on the wall depicting the signing of the Austrian State Treaty in 1955. He pointed to a figure in the second row of participants. I recognized it immediately as that of Llewellyn Thompson, the U.S. ambassador to Austria, who had been influential in the successful negotiation. "But for that man," he said, "Austria would not be free today."

After these World War II issues were resolved the world became more complex and the task of diplomacy more difficult. Patterns were established that were to influence the diplomatic techniques of the U.S. in the decades to come. New agencies were founded with their own representatives abroad, only loosely related to the traditional embassy organization. These included the United States Information Agency, the Central Intelligence Agency, and the various agencies responsible for foreign assistance. The traditional diplomats were joined by economists, planners, technicians, intelligence officers, and public affairs specialists. Diplomatic tasks were carried out against the background of an expanded bureaucracy developed to manage the many new responsibilities. Embassies became collections of representatives of ministries rather than tight families of career diplomats. Ambassadors became more referees than managers.

Statistics tell some of the story. In 1949 the United States maintained 57 embassies and legations and 288 consular posts, many in colonial territories. There were few agencies abroad other than those of the Department of State. By 1981 there were 135 embassies, 71 of them in the former colonial territories that became independent. More than 20 U.S. government agencies had representatives abroad. The Foreign Service itself expanded from 750 officers before the war to more than 3,000 by 1950.

The American diplomat in this world of wider responsibilities is subject to the contradictions of a complex society and government at home. When official messages are conveyed through American embassies, they are not likely to be either the only word or the final word on the policy. An agreement with another government may be negotiated in good faith, but Congress may fail to approve it. A statement by the Secretary of State may be contradicted in the next day's press by "an unnamed source in the administration."

The ambassador may deny U.S. involvement in a neighboring coup, but the nightly television at home may present "irrefutable proof" to the contrary. A visiting banker may dispute a promise of U.S. financial aid.

Despite these governmental complexities, one would expect the natural characteristics of Americans, their heritage of other cultures, their insatiable curiosity, and their openness to lead to effective diplomacy. Other characteristics, however, impede relations with non-Americans: national pride, insensitivity, lack of attention to the status of others, an anti-government bias, and an assumption that other societies are or ought to be a mirror image of American society. Americans have a direct approach to others: why not deal with "the people"? why let governments get in the way? In a world of nation states, however, official business must still be conducted among governments through diplomacy and by diplomats.

The American view of diplomacy is a mixture of ignorance of its details, suspicion of its objectives, contempt for its importance, and fascination with its romance. Diplomats are, in the worst of times, considered disloyal and, in the best of times, "cookie pushers." Presidents are traditionally distrustful of the Department of State—which houses diplomats. In no other major country are ambassadorships considered a primary form of political patronage. The risks and deaths of diplomats in recent years have only partially altered this view.

The American public has always had problems accepting the styles and conventions of diplomacy. To an open, impatient, assertive, action-oriented society the slow pace of diplomacy, the secretiveness, the meticulous attention to words, and the often ostentatious concern over the sensitivities of protocol serve to compound its suspicions. The natural American tendency to feel that problems can be resolved if people on opposing sides can just sit down and talk it out seems to disappear when applied to diplomacy; to sit down across the table from someone who is clearly not a friend is to confuse the black and white nature of issues and to risk giving something away. All of this leads not only to strong doubts about the art, but also to pessimism about the nation's chances of success in its diplomatic encounters.

Sir Harold Nicolson, the British diplomat, in his seminal book *Diplomacy*, has this to say about the diplomacy of the United States:

> The Americans, conversely, are convinced that all diplomatists are determined to ensnare, entangle, and humiliate all those with whom they negotiate. They enter a conference as Daniel entered the den of lions, conscious that it is only their own bright faith and innocence which will preserve them from the claws of the wild beasts by whom they are surrounded. It is in fact strange that whereas an American businessman will negotiate with foreign businessmen in a spirit of almost reckless self-confidence, an American diplomatist will, in the presence of continental diplomatists, become overwhelmed with diffidence and suspicion.

Perhaps nothing symbolizes the generally casual, if not capricious, American attitude toward diplomacy more than the process of appointing U.S. ambassadors. Representing a complex, free society such as the United States would appear to be a task requiring special skills of political and cultural sensitivity. If one looks over the several reports that have been prepared in the Congress and elsewhere on the requirements for an ambassador, the list, both in terms of personal qualities and professional skills, is long. Emphasis is placed on integrity, leadership ability, courage, discretion, intelligence, presence, and dignity. Strong recommendations are made on behalf of area knowledge, communication skills, language competency, and an understanding of the United States.

One would assume from this list of requirements that the selection of ambassadors is a comprehensive process with conscientious attention to the matching of qualifications and post requirements. This is, in general, not the case. The process more often involves bargaining between the State Department and the White House over which posts shall be "political." Decisions are likely to be more on the basis of rewards, either to politicians for their support or to foreign service officers for their longevity. Among many in the political world who assist in making the choice little understanding exists of the actual functions of an ambassador. To the stereotype of a host or hostess abroad is added the image of the personable salesperson sent abroad to make friends. The wide use of the word ambassador applied to individuals who go abroad for business, for the arts, for sports, tends to obscure the need for the person sensitized to foreign cultures who is as qualified to protect interests as to make friends.

From the time that Benjamin Franklin was appointed minister to Paris, the tradition has existed that at least a portion of U.S. diplomatic missions will be headed by persons chosen by the president from political supporters. The U.S. diplomatic service at all levels was primarily political until the enactment of the Rogers Act in 1924 established a professional foreign service. That act did not change the prerogative of presidents to appoint whom they will to be their chief representative abroad, subject only to Senate confirmation. And the Senate rarely wishes to take issue with the president's privilege to appoint whom he chooses. As a Senate staff member once said to me, "the only appointees rejected are those who have lied to the Senate."

The pressures on the White House from contributors, campaign workers, and long-time supporters, including members of Congress, either to be appointed or to have their nominees appointed are enormous. Ambassadorships are used to compensate those who cannot be accommodated with cabinet or other high level positions in Washington. In some cases, those being fired from senior positions in Washington are appointed as chiefs of mission. In such cases, the United States is not markedly different from some lesser countries that use diplomatic appointments as a way of sending troublesome political opponents abroad.

In this new age, some have even suggested that diplomats no longer mattered; either they could be dispensed with altogether or their qualifications were of less importance. Such a suggestion fails to acknowledge that, with the proliferation of U.S. agencies overseas, the leadership task of the ambassador is more complex and more important than it has ever been. To suggest that qualifications are less important ignores those moments in recent troubled history when the presence of a more qualified envoy might have seized opportunities that were otherwise lost. Occasions still arise, also, when a diplomat, out of communication with the capital, must have the skill to make crucial decisions alone. On other occasions, even if primary diplomatic communications take place between cabinet officers, someone must give them the background analysis essential for such conversations. If the U.S. diplomat is not effective, representatives of other agencies in the embassy may become more credible in Washington. The foreign government may, in such cases, conduct its serious business through its own ambassador in Washington. The U.S. ambassador, whether he or she realizes it or not, may be left out of important conversations.

The open, political approach to diplomacy was rooted in the traditions of the United States. As the United States became central to international developments, and as other democracies arose, diplomacy, generally, became more public, more open.

Nicolson, in his book *Diplomacy*, foresaw many of these changes toward "democratic diplomacy": "the irresponsibility of the people," ignorance, delay, publicity, and the participation of politicians in negotiation. He concluded, "I do not wish to leave in the mind of the reader the impression that I regard democratic diplomacy as more inefficient or dangerous than its predecessors. Far from it, I consider it, even in its present confused state, infinitely preferable to any other system. Yet I confess that, to my mind, democratic diplomacy has not yet discovered its own formula."

Nicolson wrote that in 1939. In the 1980s, in a world far more complex, the United States and, perhaps, other democracies as well were still seeking that formula.

II

$\mathscr{D}$

WHAT AMERICANS WANT
IN FOREIGN POLICY

THE CARTER AND REAGAN eras, each ideological in its way,
taught us much about ourselves.

The Carter administration had what many regarded as
diplomatic successes, yet its foreign policies were seen in the
country as failures. Much was accomplished, but each success
carried a domestic political liability. The release of the American hostages in Iran and the Camp David accord between
Israel and Egypt are two examples.

In the Iran hostage crisis nearly every known form of
diplomatic engagement and pressure was attempted including sanctions, mediation, and diplomatic isolation. Although
the hostages were ultimately all released, the protracted
efforts compounded by the abortive rescue attempt were seen
as a humiliating failure.

The agreement at Camp David was a remarkable diplomatic accomplishment that changed the strategic, military,
and political alignments in a significant corner of the world.
Yet I have repeatedly been asked, "What significant accomplishment did Carter achieve in the Middle East?" The American public seemed more prepared to criticize the Camp

David agreement because it did not achieve all that was hoped for than to applaud a diplomatic triumph.

Other examples are the SALT II and Panama Canal treaties. SALT II encountered severe opposition and was rejected by the Congress and the public even before the Soviet invasion of Afghanistan. The Carter administration concluded a Panama Canal Treaty, removing a major irritant from U.S. relations with Latin America. That treaty was immediately attacked; it passed through the Senate only after some difficult further negotiations with Panama. The normalization of relations with China, the foundations of which were laid in the Nixon administration, brought not praise, but the additional complications of the Taiwan Relations Act.

Officials of the Carter administration played an important role in the transformation of isolated Rhodesia into independent Zimbabwe, removing a major issue from the international agenda. British diplomacy ultimately resolved the problem, but the effective groundwork laid by Secretary of State Cyrus Vance, Ambassador Andrew Young, Anthony Lake, Richard Moose, and others made the resolution possible.

Despite these achievements in foreign affairs, Jimmy Carter was an unpopular president. In contrast, there have been fewer similar accomplishments in the Reagan administration, but Ronald Reagan has been more popular because he has more effectively responded to what Americans want in foreign policy.

The pendulum of emphases in American diplomacy and in American policy swings widely depending on political developments and international events. The swings are between stress on security versus stress on peace—as in the endless debate on arms control agreements with the Soviet Union— or between withdrawing from the world or remaking it. As the London *Economist* remarked in an article on January 21, 1984, "At one extreme, the United States ignores the world outside the Americas because it feels it neither likes it nor needs it. At the other, it plunges into the world to put it to rights."

Foreign affairs and diplomacy are domestic political— often partisan—questions in the United States. There is no recognition of diplomacy as a part of "the state," above politics, as in many European countries. Americans apply their basic suspicion of authority and rejection of government to those who conduct foreign affairs as they do to those with domestic responsibilities. Viewing relations with other nations through the immutable circumstances of their history and geography, Americans value the heritage of detachment from the quarrels of Europe and reject the concept of balance of power. Political campaigns, in their exaggerated way, proclaim these attitudes to a listening and watching world.

Americans take pride in their country, even though at times they recoil from what seems to be a high degree of emotion and chauvinism in the politics of other countries. The display of the flag, a Fourth of July parade, the homecoming of hostages, and a stirring patriotic speech bring out the exuberance of the American people. As a diplomat, I have had chills run down my spine on many occasions when the American flag has been raised in foreign countries, an American ship has sailed into a harbor, or the prompt contribution by my country of help to disaster victims has been recognized.

The United States is also a sensitive country. Many abroad have felt that they could disguise criticism of their own lands by attacking the United States. They assumed that Americans were tolerant to the point of turning the other cheek. They have been surprised at indignant U.S. reactions and at evidence that Americans are sensitive to such criticism.

Pride and sensitivity mean that Americans are concerned with their prestige in the world. On many occasions, debates in the United States on policies and actions have revolved around the degree to which either will represent "weakness." In such cases, the perception of weakness may be solely within the American mind, evidence of a not-so-latent machismo, or may be encouraged by foreigners who look to the United States for their own security. Most nations probably prefer restraint and patience on the part of a great power over dramatic demonstrations of strength.

But restraint does not come easily to Americans. The United States, justifiably, sees itself as a global power; some call it "imperialist." It has difficulty relating to other countries as equals. Its military commands are organized to stretch around the world. Security responsibilities are assumed for regions of the world without consultation with the countries of the region. Manifest destiny is not dead.

Americans tend to see both peace and strength largely in military terms. The traditions of the frontier reinforce the idea that military power brings respect. Americans believe that their country had fewer difficulties in the field of foreign relations when it had superior military power in the 1950s. Such events as the invasion of Hungary, the nationalization of the Suez Canal, and the Iraqi Revolution, all of which had a profound effect upon American interests, are largely forgotten. Americans talk in the 1980s about regaining a power that they never fully had.

Americans must be number one. The intense spirit of competitiveness at home carries over into the approach to diplomacy. Americans do not want merely to adjust to other nations; they want "to win." No one fully understands the United States who does not understand the American passion for sports. Americans believe in the need for superior power. If it has been lost, it must be regained. If the United States is not number one, something should be done to make it so. Ronald Reagan appealed to this deep feeling, but it existed well before him.

Americans see the world in terms of friendship, not in terms of interests—perhaps because it is difficult to define or to reach a consensus on what constitutes national interests. When speaking to an audience in the United States, to suggest that the international relations should be built on interests rather than friendship is to risk a severe challenge, if not a reprimand. Friendship is defined not only in terms of the attitudes of other countries toward the Soviet Union, but also in terms of cooperation and friendly rhetoric. Americans divide the world between "those on our side" and those "not on our side." They have trouble accepting the neutral nation, especially one that appears to consider the United States as only one among many. Nations become unpopular by failing to accept American leadership or, what is worse, by equating the United States with the Soviet Union. Americans freely use labels like pro-American, pro-Soviet, moderate, extreme, neutral, but become confused when states thought of as moderate link up with those considered extremist. Americans become even more confused when friends do not fully support U.S. policies or share U.S. views on major issues. Again and again in my career, whether discussing a country with visiting members of Congress overseas or with audiences at home, the questions have come: "Whose side are they on? Are they for us or against us?" All of this relates to the central preoccupation of most Americans: the confrontation with the Soviets.

While other nations tend to regard the Soviet Union as one of the superpowers or as just another nation, the U.S. attitude is a mixture of fear and curiosity. The fear is specifically of the Soviet Union, the one nation that has the military power to threaten America. The fear is also of the communist philosophy that if given a chance to flourish, many Americans believe, will take away that which they as individuals and as a nation have gained in material wealth and personal freedom.

The American attitude toward the Soviet Union needs also to be understood in the light of the expectations after World War II. The experience of other wars had led Americans to believe that once the war was concluded there would be peace. Armies could be demobilized and the country could resume its position of relatively detached isolation. The shock of the Soviet incorporation of Eastern Europe and other evidences of a very different and hostile Soviet view of the world made a profound imprint on U.S. thinking. The period after World War II brought a substantial flow of peoples to the United States from Eastern Europe. Their attitudes toward the Soviet Union, to a large extent, remained frozen by their view of postwar circumstances, of Stalin, and of the Soviet power in Eastern Europe. They have heavily influenced U.S. political and strategic thinking. Their static views are often in stark contrast to those who remained behind in their former homelands and see the Soviet Union in more current and less rigid terms.

No politician can afford to challenge this central national preoccupation with the Soviet Union. In his famous 1976 debate with Jimmy Carter, President Gerald Ford's statement that there is "no Soviet domination of Eastern Europe" *(New York Times,* October 7, 1976) probably cost him the election. Similarly, Carter's statement after the invasion of Afghanistan that the action "made a more dramatic change in my own opinion of what the Soviets ultimate goals are than anything they've done in the previous time . . ." *(New York Times,* June 1, 1980) probably did him an equal amount of political harm.

Political statements about other countries pose a special risk for American politicians because the United States is a nation of immigrants. Throughout its history, people have been fleeing to America from disasters or oppression, carrying with them the fears, prejudices, and ambitions of that trek.

The *Economist* article quoted above puts it this way:

> The American view of the world is different from the European view, because the Americans' history has made them into a different sort of people.
> The Americans are not, as too many Europeans think they are, a collection of intermarried Europeans who happen to have moved sideways across the Atlantic, plus some blacks and hispanics. They are the descendants, in overwhelming majority, of

people who left Europe because they wanted to be free or rich
and the old world kept them squashed and poor, so they shook
Europe's dust off their feet.

Having shaken off the dust of other countries, Americans
reject all but the cultural anachronisms of the place from
which they came. Those whose family lines have been longest
in the new world stress ideals of the founding fathers and the
legends of continental expansion. Those who have come more
recently from regions of trouble or oppression bring with
them a fear they cannot fully shake. This inherent sense of
flight from former perils gives the impression, at times, that
American is a frightened nation—in the reaction to terrorism
abroad, in the passion for a minimum of risk in our international actions. Part of the fear lies in America's distance from
many of the events; proximity can sometimes put events in
less extreme perspectives.

Whatever their origins, Americans believe that their country is special. Whether descendants of early settlers or new-
comers, Americans believe there is no place like the United
States of America. They are reinforced in this belief by their
awareness of the many in other lands still dreaming of coming to America. Not without justification, they feel that the
United States has made unique contributions to the world in
political philosophy, democracy, generosity. The freedom created, espoused, and embodied in the nation's democratic institutions is at the heart of this conviction. A belief, perhaps
not always openly declared, exists that the world, if it is to be
peaceful and free, should ultimately conform to the paths that
Americans have charted and create institutions on the American model.

Americans believe especially that the United States is
more generous and unselfish than other nations. They are
proud of U.S. responses to humanitarian disasters, and while
U.S. foreign assistance programs are not large or popular,
Americans still refer to them as an indication of their gener-

osity. In so doing, they gloss over the paradoxes of lower levels of U.S. assistance compared to other nations, the unfulfilled expectations, and the mixed reactions of the world to the spread of American culture.

As one author, discussing "the American idea of nation," commented: "Non-Americans surely have cause to find American nationalism more than a little annoying. What is one to make of a big, strong, wealthy country whose citizens are constantly congratulating themselves on how exceptional they are—their historic mission, 'city-on-a-hillishness,' special political virtues, their immense good fortune in history's crap-shoot or, even more, their divine ordination?" (Everett Carll Ladd, in the *Christian Science Monitor*, September 30, 1985).

The combination of competitiveness, desire for action, and sense of mission makes the American restless and impatient. When an American diplomat takes a new issue or development to a Secretary of State or to one of his aides, the question is not likely to be, "What are the facts? Do we need to do something?" It is more apt to be, "What are we going to do about it?" The open political system presses for immediate and action-related responses.

Diplomacy can be slow. Protracted negotiations are seen as a sign of weakness. Americans are suspicious of such a prolonged process, particularly when there may not be a clear idea of the outcome. They are still deeply affected by the fact that the major efforts this country made in World War I and World War II resulted relatively quickly in forms of unconditional surrender. Vietnam showed many things, but it showed, above all, the unwillingness of the United States as a nation to endure a protracted conflict without a clear prospect of victory. If Americans are impatient, they are also optimistic. Europeans see history as a struggle; Americans see history as a constant progression to something better. Foreign policy is often seen in negative terms because it seems to permit others to place obstacles in the path of progress.

Every problem has a solution, preferably a quick one. The quick military option is preferred over labored diplomacy. The U.S. public cheered the *Mayaguez* capture in 1975, the Grenada invasion in 1983, and the capture of the hijackers of the *Achille Lauro* in 1985. They were far less enthusiastic over the prolonged negotiations for the release of the hostages in Iran in 1980.

Two events involving Libya illustrate differences between the reaction of the United States and that of the United Kingdom. When Libyans fired out of the People's Bureau in London in 1984, killing a London policewoman, the British talked with the Libyans, they confined their reaction to a single incident, they limited comments to a non-political level, they made no military moves, and the British community remained in Libya. Terrorist acts involving the deaths of Americans in Europe brought military action against Libya, strong statements from President Reagan, and soaring public support for the president's action.

A diplomatic effort in the United States must have a broad national consensus and be credible in terms of the national capacity and interests. Because such efforts are at times taken to satisfy a domestic political requirement that seems insignificant in world terms, foreigners often ask why U.S. actions seem disproportionate to the nation's real interests.

Nothing is more unpopular with Americans than the suggestion that there are some problems that cannot be resolved but only managed. But here there is a complex set of paradoxes. They believe "talking" is good in a conflict situation, yet are suspicious of negotiation. They can be bellicose in rhetoric yet cautious in the use of military action. They have a romantic belief in covert action, yet are suspicious of secrets.

To Americans, the absence of a solution to an international problem suggests failure; someone must be responsible. I have appeared as a witness before congressional committees seeking information about revolutions in which U.S. interests were involved. I have inevitably been asked why we did not know the revolution was coming and do something to prevent it.

Americans believe that order is the normal state of society because they have created it in their country. They tend to favor the status quo, whatever it is, and to be upset by revolutionary change, while constantly stimulating change. Peace in the world is a strong rhetorical objective because Americans believe that to be the normal state of the world despite their own Civil War; they have difficulty conceiving of those who consider peace secondary to other objectives. The American view of the world embraces both combative and benign tendencies.

The benign view is illustrated by the assumption that "Everyone basically is really like us." Ultimately logic will prevail in any international situation, and that logic obviously will lead people to agree with the United States. Americans believe not only that people in the world want peace, but also that economic considerations will ultimately outweigh political or emotional considerations. They believe that people are fundamentally good-hearted and that others share the Americans' humanitarian instincts. Likewise, they are certain that others seek democracy as they have done.

A strong, almost religious, belief exists in free enterprise, a belief that comes naturally out of a country built on the risks and motivations of the free enterprise system. There is a distinct fear of the term "socialism." In the firm and justifiable belief in the merits of the free enterprise system as it has worked in the United States, Americans gain an inadequate view of the different conditions in other countries, whether developed or developing, that have led to different systems and different attitudes. The story of America's own national development is romanticized. Free enterprise is seen as a pattern that should automatically be adaptable to other countries. In celebrating America's economic success, such advantages as the assistance it received from other nations, the richness of its natural resources, and its relatively small population are largely forgotten.

The U.S. diplomat is frequently forced to challenge these tenets by pointing out that the motivations of individuals in the Middle East, China, or Central America may be quite different from the motivations of individuals in the United States. In Lebanon, for example, the desire for revenge, fear of slaughter, or deep historic antagonisms may prevail over any desire for peace. Arab concern over profits from the sale of oil did not prevent the imposition of an oil embargo in 1973. Humanitarian considerations for the people of Biafra in the Nigerian civil war of 1969-71 were secondary to the national pride and sense of sovereignty in Lagos.

Blind spots exist in the Americans' capacity to assess other societies because of tendencies to assume parallel motives and to hear what they want to hear. They become vulnerable to the nation or the person who appeals for help on American terms, but who may have quite a different objective. The professed anticommunist may be much more interested in besting a neighbor, the vocal capitalist more interested in establishing a personal monopoly. A failure to look behind statements from foreigners for the real motive often leads to decisions and actions based on highly erroneous expectations and assessments. Time and again the United States has entered arrangements abroad with one objective while those collaborating with them had another. Iraq joined the anti-Soviet Baghdad Pact in 1955 in the hope of gaining U.S. support for the Arab cause against Israel. Pakistan sought U.S. arms ostensibly to defend against the Soviets, but the threat from India was a much greater motive. Israel persuaded the United States to supply arms to Iran on the pretext of helping the U.S. open channels to Khomeini; the deeper motive was to defeat Iraq. For nations to enter a common arrangement with different purposes is not unknown; for one partner to appear to be oblivious to the true designs of the other is rarer.

Such delusions are easier in dealing with authoritarian regimes where vocal parliamentarians will not complicate the relationship. Ironically, Americans want a world that is

democratic and yet they have difficulty relating to other democracies. In Latin America and in Asia, U.S. policies have
frequently found more support from authoritarian regimes.
Democracies tend too often to challenge U.S. assumptions
about the rest of the world. The United States has rarely had
periods of good relations with the world's largest democracy,
India.

Each of these American attitudes has implications for the
relations of the United States with the separate regions of the
world. Neither Europe, more united now than ever, nor
Japan, with its aggressive economy, accepts the U.S. claim to
be number one. Europe has a different view of the Soviet
Union and of socialism. They look upon foreign policy as
based more on interests than on friendships. In other parts of
the world, particularly in Central America and the Middle
East, while the economic and political power of the United
States may be recognized, there is less acknowledgement of
U.S. preeminence and the U.S. ability to control events. America began to discover even in the 1960s that its power had
limitations. The United States could not control events,
whether in Hungary, Czechoslovakia, Iraq, Egypt, or even on
the nation's doorstep in Cuba. There were other players, not
all of whom were communists or declared adversaries.

In many ways the American diplomat abroad was among
the first to become conscious that the United States, despite
its power, was less capable of shaping events than many in
Washington anticipated and expected. Regional powers such
as India and Brazil exerted influence that made the United
States less relevant in the region. The Economic Community
in Europe had a life and mind of its own; it came as a shock to
American diplomats to be excluded from meetings of EC
ambassadors.

There are, of course, variations in attitudes toward the
United States by region, by race, by background. Among
friends and allies in all continents the United States has
staunch defenders, even if at times they are bewildered by

events in Washington. Whatever these variations, the policies the United States pursues, whether radical or imaginative or cautious, must, to be acceptable, be expressed and explained and defended to skeptical, distracted, and occasionally unfriendly governments and peoples abroad. This becomes the task of the American diplomat who, in a mediating role, must also explain the realities that confront America to those in Washington who may be unready to accept the anomalies of an outside world. The U.S. diplomat does so against a background of national attitudes often at variance from those of the rest of the world and for a nation traditionally skeptical, if not suspicious, of the role and tasks of diplomacy.

III

☙

WASHINGTON

WHEN I WAS FIRST named an ambassador (to Libya, in 1965) my wife and I were invited, with six other couples, to meet President Lyndon Johnson. The president met the group in the Oval Office, and in rapid succession we were each photographed with him. We were then escorted to the Rose Garden where he talked about our assignments. It was the only time in my career that a president gave me a "charge." I have not forgotten it.

After saying a few words about the importance he attached to the country's foreign relations, the president said, in his distinct Texas drawl, "Now, if you get out to where you're going and you don't like it there, please let me know. I'll bring you home, because I don't want any of you messin' me up."

Presidents for whom I have worked have, in one way or another, manifested a concern about how they and the nation are perceived abroad. They have looked to their diplomatic representatives to advise them, although not all have welcomed what diplomats had to say. As the interpreter between two societies, the diplomat must not only understand a foreign society, but must also be able to convey insights on that

24

society to leaders at home who are, understandably, preoccupied with domestic and political considerations.

In the diplomacy of any country, there are moments when a diplomat has difficulty describing a situation to the ministers or secretaries in the capital. A Soviet Ambassador no doubt has problems when he describes the "chaos" of a democracy to those in Moscow conditioned by totalitarian rule. Ambassadors in Washington from Third World countries, many of whom are in "exile" as political rivals, must try credibly to explain American indifference to a small country. Even European ambassadors in the United States may not be fully understood when they try to explain to their home offices the relationship between the Congress and the executive.

These problems are no greater, however, than those of a U.S. diplomat seeking to make the system of another political society understandable to U.S. officials. The American diplomat stands or falls on the ability to manage that distant relationship between the political and bureaucratic structure in a capital and the embassy abroad. This requires an understanding of the policy making process at home and the skill to explain to those involved in that process developments in a very different and possibly incomprehensible foreign environment.

To the politician, the diplomat attempting to explain another country can seem strongly parochial. Under the emotional strain of existence in an area of high tension and conflict, such as the Middle East, diplomats can lose their balance and their credibility. The diplomat who, by speech and manner, suggests that officials in Washington are uninformed or unappreciative of the important role of a foreign country is likely to be reminded that he or she is representing the United States, not the other country. Many Americans, sensitive to the political currents of their own country, seem strangely unable to recognize that foreign leaders also have domestic political pressures. The Washington preference is for the diplomat who is "tough," who speaks bluntly and candidly to foreigners.

It is said that diplomacy is not political. Many diplomats seek to avoid any intimation that they are part of a political process. But diplomacy is intensely political. The difference is that the diplomat exists in a multicultural world while the traditional politician in the United States or elsewhere exists in a more definable domestic setting. The realms are quite different, although each is, in its way, political. The diplomat abroad, in projecting the interests of a country, is seeking to persuade the hosts to make political decisions that are often difficult, if not dangerous, for them. Supporting the policies of the United States in some parts of the world requires great courage; both political and personal risks are involved.

In Washington, as in most capitals, the primary interest of the national leadership is to manage foreign affairs in a way that will do the least damage to a government's domestic standing. Perceptions of national interest are shaped by the politician's reading of what the public wants and will tolerate. They are shaped, also, in the United States by the political time spans, those periods of two, four, or six years between elections. Diplomats must be able to read the political signals at home if they are to influence the policy process.

Built into any democratic political system are serious obstacles to the orderly conduct of diplomacy. Political campaigns often involve rhetoric that is offensive to other nations and pledges of commitments in foreign policy that may be difficult or impossible to implement, at least without damage to the normal relationships with others. Changes in administration, especially if they represent an abrupt change in ideology, mean that history is reinvented and institutional memory destroyed. The career official who attempts to remind the new team of what has gone before may lose credibility. Even more unpopular is the suggestion that the reality of the world may in time dawn upon the new leadership and create policies little different from those of the preceding administration.

American diplomats have been required, through several administrations, to explain to foreigners not only changes in policies, but also the many and often conflicting voices of the policy process. Countries heavily dependent on the United States for political, military, or economic support will search for signals in rhetoric, in appointments, and in proposals that may give clues to the true direction of U.S. policy. There can be little doubt that countries such as South Africa, South Korea, the Philippines (under Marcos), and Argentina (under military rule) were encouraged by the shift from Carter to Reagan to believe that the pressures on them for reform would be reduced. Similarly, right-wing elements in Central America hoped for strong support and were at times encouraged by voices from the United States peripheral to the policy process. Efforts of U.S. diplomats to explain the wider considerations that might prevent drastic changes in policies toward these countries were greeted with skepticism.

Whether from the career Foreign Service or appointed from outside, the U.S. diplomat must build up credibility that will make messages from an embassy influential, effective, and meaningful. Traditionally, the professional has the greater difficulty because, by nature, the politicians and their staffs influential in the creation of policy harbor doubts toward those who have served loyally in a previous administration. In the case of ideological administrations, such as the Carter and Reagan administrations, the degree of suspicion is deep and the task of establishing credibility that much greater. The problem has been compounded in the Reagan administration by the expectation that ambassadors will promote in the countries in which they serve not only the foreign policy, but the particular ideological viewpoint of a president as well.

Most U.S. diplomats spend a portion of their career in the

Washington bureaucracy. Some rise to positions that are, in effect, political. To the diplomat fresh from the field, the Washington experience initially can appear chaotic. There is, however, a certain order within that chaos. To the newcomer, no one seems to be in charge in Washington. The effort to learn where power lies is complicated by the game of personalities. Washington cocktail parties thrive on the debate over the hierarchy of personalities. Who is really on top: the Secretary of State, the Secretary of Defense, the National Security Advisor? The argument is perpetual. The policymaking phenomenon is part of a complex government structure and of the balance of forces inherent in the Constitution. The Constitution gives some powers to the president and some powers to the Congress in a way that has at times been called "an invitation to struggle."

The diplomat in Washington first views the process from the perspective of the Department of State. In that department, the feeling is strong that primary responsibility for foreign affairs should lie with the Secretary of State. The diplomat then discovers there are many other players.

The answer to the question of who is in charge is clear, or should be. It is the president of the United States. But the neophyte learns that the matter is not that simple. One has to ask who advises the president, who briefs him first on issues, who may see him last, who drafts the last piece of paper on the file that requires his decision. Who is located most closely to him and sees him with greater ease and greater frequency? The secretary of state is always at a built-in disadvantage because he is several blocks away from the White House and is frequently traveling or defending policy on Capitol Hill.

But it would be wrong to see policy making only or primarily as a contest for personal power. Egos are involved, but so are strong beliefs: What is good for the nation? What is good politically for an administration? For the individuals in the policy process, whether political appointees or professionals, high risks are involved. Political life is ever vulnerable. The American tendency to assess blame for what may be inevitable means that those in the policy process are concerned about responsibility for disasters, about the vulnerability to blame. It is not enough to say that the Chinese lost China or the Iranians lost Iran. In the eyes of many Americans, someone in an administration must have failed to do what was needed.

The issues that men and women in government face today are momentous. They involve peace and war and the preservation of a major nation. They involve decisions on the use of enormous military strength. They embrace questions of economics that affect the lives of people around the world. They relate to the exercise of American diplomatic influence toward the resolution of other critical world issues. They involve the projection of American ideals through concerns over human rights, over the institutions of other governments, and over problems of political change. Those in Washington must reconcile these various interests in the elaborate budget process and in the establishment of priorities for the utilization of resources. All of this goes forward under the scrutiny of Congress and the media and against the backdrop of great expectations from friends, criticism from restless allies, and challenges from adversaries. In many cases there are no simple answers; there are only unpleasant alternatives.

In the debates that surround the creation of policies, individuals gain a vested interest in the success of their position. This applies especially to contentious issues such as those involving relations with the Soviet Union, including the highly complex issues of arms control, actions in Central America, countering the Cuban presence in Africa, and matters of trade and finance. Diplomatic messages are read by advocates and opponents of policy in Washington. Those who send them and act upon them are judged for their adherence or loyalty to one side or another of factional divisions within the nation's capitol. One hears constantly in Washington the expressed desire for a more rational process leading to clear policies and instructions to diplomats, but the process does not permit this. A clear national strategy, so often recommended, does not emerge from the hectic game of adjustment that moves the American democracy.

Diplomats also become involved in the bureaucratic contest to control consultations with significant foreign governments. Which departments or personalities will conduct major policy discussions with the Russians or with the principal allies? To what extent will the normal diplomatic discussions be preempted by "back channel" traffic between the National Security Council staff and counterpart offices in Europe. Europeans sometimes complain at the lack of consultation with the United States. At times the problem is an excess of consultation through several channels, any one of which may be unaware of the other.

Whatever the technological advances, diplomats are at the end of a fragile line of communication. Their success will depend upon the ability to interpret what is received from the capital and to respond in a way that is accurate, printable, and attentive to the needs of the government.

As an example, Washington likes to deal at the top. In some cases, U.S. officials in Washington judge the effectiveness of an American ambassador by noting the degree to which that ambassador has access to the head of state. Even if not explicitly instructed, the diplomat learns to assume that Washington expects that most important matters will be raised with the head of government, the prime minister, or the foreign minister. In relations with major governments, there is a practical reason for this insistence. When papers proceed through a bureaucracy, other interests may wish to sidetrack the proposed approach or may seek to interpret a message in ways that change its meaning or diminish its effectiveness. In the case of smaller countries the assumption is that only people at the top will understand the message and make the proper decision. This presents the American diplomat with problems. Some countries insist on reciprocity. If Nigeria's ambassador in Washington cannot regularly see the president or secretary of state, why should access to comparable senior officials in Lagos be given to the U.S. ambassador? It is the rare foreign diplomat in Washington who can see the president or even regularly see the secretary of state. Unless the United States enjoys a special position in a country, foreign governments are reluctant to grant access to a U.S. ambassador lest they establish a precedent upon which other ambassadors will insist. Appointments secretaries of senior foreign officials abroad are as diligent in protecting access to their principals as their counterparts in Washington.

Then there is the question of "using up currency." Even in countries where the U.S. ambassador may have access to a head of state or head of government, the foreign officials will expect that privilege to be used sparingly. If they see the U.S. ambassador too often, they will be under pressure to accord the same access to others. In the case of President Suharto of Indonesia, for example, it became clear that he would receive the American ambassador only if the ambassador were bringing a message from the president of the United States or a visitor of high status. Any ambassador must carefully judge how often and under what circumstances to seek appointments with leading officials, whatever may be the instructions from Washington.

Washington is, however, not sympathetic to arguments from an embassy that the ambassador is being pressed to spend currency too freely. Ambassadors must therefore find ways to satisfy Washington that the message reaches the highest levels of government even if an appointment at the moment with the head of state or the minister is not possible. An ambassador's relationship with the special assistant or a close associate of a senior official then becomes important.

A related question is whether sensitive messages should be sent through the American ambassador abroad or through the ambassador of the country in Washington. In recent years this argument involved the long-time Soviet ambassador in

Washington, Anatoly Dobrynin.* As a member of the Central Committee of the Communist Party, Dobrynin was believed by most secretaries of state to have more direct access to the Soviet leadership than officials in the foreign ministry with whom the ambassador in Moscow would ordinarily deal. In such cases the ambassador of the United States in the capital abroad is placed in the uncomfortable position of being less aware of the activities and policies of his own government than those at the top of the host country.

A skillful ambassador will seek to determine why messages are sent from Washington. Documents do not necessarily mean what they say. The ambassador is foolish who regards instructions from the capital as immutable holy writ—who rushes to the Foreign Office to convey the message in exactly the form in which it was sent.

Messages sent from a nation's capital are couched in language that will ensure the maximum concurrence by all of the variety of bureaucratic and political players involved. The Department of State may occasionally send a message to satisfy the internal pressures of the moment, but with the hope that the ambassador, correctly reading this fact, will either rephrase the instructions to prevent an adverse reaction from the local government or in some skillful way suggest to Washington that the instructions should be amended. An ambassador aware of the context of policy and events in Washington should be able to determine the true intent of a message. It may well be, "We know this is difficult for you but do what you can." Still other messages may be correctly read as being "for the record." Between the lines is the instruction, "Do what you can but don't break the china." In such cases the ambassador will find the least troublesome way to convey the message to the local government. Responding to Washington is as much of a game as reading the messages. Even highly restricted incoming messages may circulate to as

*Dobrynin returned to Moscow in 1985 to assume a position as Foreign Affairs Adviser in the Central Committee of the Communist Party.

many as a hundred different addressees in Washington. This increases the possibility of leaks; it also increases the possibility of critical assessments of the ambassador's response. Other members of the embassy staff including the military attachés, the intelligence officers, the commercial officers, and information personnel have their own channels to Washington. The diplomat will be aware that the response he or she is sending will be read in conjunction with other assessments from the post. Messages from elements in an embassy may be sent through other "back channels" of which the ambassador may not even be aware. The problem becomes acute in dealing with issues in which there is a division within the embassy itself or in which the assessment from the field may be counter to that held by important elements in Washington.

At times the divisions within Washington and between Washington and an embassy in the field have become so acute that special emissaries have been sent to the field, either to reinforce a particular point of view or to bring an embassy into line. During the Nigerian Civil War, for example, when there was a major policy dispute between the U.S. embassy in Lagos, interested in maintaining relations with the Federal Military Government, and those in the White House promoting humanitarian relief to Biafra, a team from the National Security Council was sent to Lagos to reprimand the embassy and to try to bring the reporting from that post more in line with administration thinking.

The most dramatic clash of the political and diplomatic cultures comes during high-level visits abroad, particularly presidential visits. Whatever may be the president's personal view of the visit abroad, his staff is likely to see it largely as one more event in the chief executive's domestic political campaign. The concerns of the staff are how the president will appear, photo opportunities, and a schedule that meets the requirements of U.S. television. Foreign relations become secondary. Diplomacy suffers from the brashness and demands of presidential advance parties and, during a visit, when the American security detail and those handling the press push officials of the host country out of the way so that the president may be at the center of the stage.

Comparable shocks occur during official visits of foreign leaders to Washington. American practices do not match either the expectations or practices of foreign governments. Strict limits exist on what the U.S. government will pay for; these are made known to the advance parties. There are no VIP lounges in New York's John F. Kennedy International Airport, a key port of entry for foreign officials. Lesser officials included in a visiting party who consider themselves important, too, are left on their own. U.S. diplomats accompanying such parties must try to smooth the rough edges. Many a diplomat has lost the battle to preserve some semblance of courtesy and has fallen by the wayside in the perilous moments of a high-level visit.

U.S. foreign policy positions are often the result of difficult negotiations among bureaucratic elements, each one sensitive to the inclusion of its point of view. When a particularly important instruction is sent to the field an ambassador knows the importance of covering all points of the instruction and reporting this fact in detail to Washington. Sometimes much less attention is paid to the response of the foreign official; some serious misunderstandings have resulted because the reply seems less important than the fact that the carefully crafted American points of view have been transmitted. A nod or a noncommittal reply may be interpreted, in the absence of a clear "no," as assent.

One of the greatest challenges open to an American ambassador is dealing with the unthinkable. When U.S. diplomats challenge policy assumptions in their reporting, they often encounter the tendency of some officials only to hear that which supports their point of view. Many times my colleagues and I have reported to Washington that a regime may be in trouble or that conflict is likely, only to be told that another source equally important to the policymaker has taken a different point of view. An embassy has—or should have—a comprehensive view of the major sectors of another society, its strengths and its weaknesses. Diplomats know this may be unpalatable to leaders in the capital who prefer the voices of others to whom they are committed or who tell them what they want to hear. No one likes to face the possibility that the policies they have advocated may turn out to be wrong.

Being aware that different points of view may exist in Washington, an American ambassador needs to build a credibility that prepares government leaders for surprises. This can be done by careful reporting of changing circumstances, including quotes from other sources in the country acceptable to Washington and by repeated reminders of the fragile nature of a local situation. To be effective, these must be accompanied by reassurances that the ambassador is aware of the problems as seen from Washington and of the existence of other assessments.

Washington does not encourage challenges to conventional wisdom. Nevertheless, although officials may temporarily welcome the ambassador who seems to agree with the prevailing political climate in the United States, that attitude quickly turns sour when it is revealed that the ambassador may have had other views but was unwilling to send them forward because of his or her apprehension about how they would be received. Communicating with the nation's capital is a perilous business for American envoys. That peril in the long run is less when the communications are totally honest but conveyed in the context of an understanding of the complexities and sensitivities of the policymaking process.

I V

⚘

DIPLOMATS AND
THE CONGRESS

IN MOST DEMOCRATIC COUNTRIES, the parliament watches over the diplomatic process—but its power is peripheral. In the United States, the Congress is part of the action. When a U.S.diplomat sits down across the table from an experienced foreign official to discuss or to negotiate, both the foreign official and the American are likely to be conscious of another presence, that of the Congress of the United States. The Constitution provides the Congress the power to appropriate money, regulate commerce, declare war, and raise and support armies. The president has the power to appoint ambassadors and negotiate treaties, subject to the advice and consent of the Senate. Between these somewhat narrowly defined areas, Congress has filled a vacuum that influences, limits, and occasionally conflicts with the orderly process of American diplomacy.

As a consequence, Congress, through its legislative review and ratification processes, the practice of hearings, and the free expressions and peripatetic activities of individual members, affects the implementation of foreign policy in ways unparalleled in any other country. In no other major nation does the diplomat face the same kinds of legislative involvement. In a parliamentary system, even one with a coalition government, acts of parliament or of individual members in contravention of agreed policy are rare.

To be thoroughly honest in a negotiation, an American diplomat is obligated to explain that the results of the negotiation may at a minimum be subject to congressional review or, in the case of a treaty, to the uncertain and domestically oriented process of ratification. American diplomats, in a circumstance rare on the world stage, are in no position to assure a foreign negotiator that what may have been agreed upon will be accepted by the U.S. government.

If money is the issue, any commitment made will be subject to the lengthy authorization and appropriations process. Statements in diplomatic discussions regarding levels of economic assistance, for example, can only be approximations, at best, of what the United States might do—until Congress has acted.

In presenting official policy, the U.S. diplomat is conscious that congressional views may be quite different from those of the administration even if Congress is controlled by the president's party. The representatives in Washington of other countries will be reporting these divergent views. The differences may be emblazoned on the front page of foreign newspapers. Individual members of Congress, in touch with foreign diplomats, may also be conveying contrary signals. The credibility of the official expressions of U.S. diplomats is subject constantly to the challenge of congressional views.

The atmosphere as well as the substance of a negotiation can be affected by comments on the issue or the country made by individual members of Congress or by witnesses questioned in hearings. More than one U.S. ambassador has been diverted from official instructions by the need to explain some unexpected outburst in Congress.

It is not surprising, then, that when foreign offices around the world assess what they will do in response to a request from the United States, officials will read both the executive and legislative expressions and ask themselves, "Which one will prevail?"

An American diplomat abroad can try to explain the separation of powers and the ultimate responsibility of the president and the secretary of state for the conduct of foreign policy. In my experience, few foreign officials, even in democracies, fully understand or accept the apparent limits on presidential power. Some will recall the congressional role at the end of the Vietnam war, but they may see it as an aberration. Efforts to explain the congressional role are frequently seen by foreign officials as lame excuses for the unwillingness of the U.S. president to respond adequately to the needs of a foreign friend.

Members of Congress abroad sometimes make an effort to lessen the confusion. I was always grateful to the late Senator Theodore Green of Rhode Island who, with a delegation of other senators, visited Pakistan in 1948, not long after that new nation was born. I was the information officer in the embassy. Senator Green came to me and said, "I would imagine that the officials of this new nation, established in the British tradition, are not aware of some of the complexities of our own government. If you would like to set up a meeting, I would be glad to try to explain something of the role of the Senate in foreign affairs." I did so. Senator Green gave a splendid explanation of the position of the Senate in appointments, appropriations, and treaty making.

But that was long ago. He could speak of the role of a Senate cooperating with the executive in such major initiatives as the North Atlantic Treaty, the Truman Doctrine for Greece and Turkey, and the Marshall Plan. In the intervening years, the line between executive and congressional responsibility in matters touching diplomacy has become more and more blurred. It is questionable whether any of the major treaties negotiated after World War II could be ratified today.

The blurring of that line has increased as communication,

consultation, and confidence between the Congress and the executive have declined. The growing frequency of leaks of sensitive information by both advocates and dissenters and the fragmentation of the organization of Congress have created opportunities to exploit serious differences in policy in both branches.

The purist in diplomacy will frequently be critical, if not resentful, of the congressional role. Such attitudes complicate, often severely, the essential dialogue with the Congress on matters affecting our diplomatic communication with other countries. The congressional role is a fact of life not likely to be substantially altered without a fundamental change in our form of democracy.

A strong consensus in the Congress, even when not in support of official policy, can help diplomacy. Pointing to such a consensus can help explain and make credible the difficulties a president may have in pursuing a specific policy. U.S. diplomats are not apt to be successful in convincing other nations of the sincerity or workability of policies or in persuading them to make difficult decisions if they fail to take note of the expressions of Congress. At the same time, diplomacy cannot be hostage to congressional views.

Administrations at times will seek through diplomacy to press objectives in the face of clearly contrary congressional signals. As recent history has shown, in such cases as SALT II and the Panama Canal treaty, this course is perilous. At the same time, administrations may determine that the national interest gives them little choice but to pursue an agreement, despite such signals. In such cases, a president is often reinforced by the possibility that the expression of Congress can be reversed. History has demonstrated that there is no certain way to know the ultimate will of Congress before an agreement is actually submitted for review. The SALT II treaty failed, but the Panama Canal treaty, despite heavy opposition, was ultimately ratified—although only after further negotiations with Panama dictated by congressional pressure.

In a discussion of these two treaties, I put to three former members of the Senate Foreign Relations Committee five suggestions of ways that the sense of the Senate might be established during the process of negotiation:

1. Through having members of the Senate as observers on the delegation;

2. Through having staff members in liaison with the delegation;

3. Through a "sense of the Senate resolution" outlining the general limits of acceptable conditions—to be passed before the negotiations start;

4. Through a pause in the negotiations at which time members of a delegation might return for discussions with the relevant committees;

5. Through periodic visits of the pertinent committees to the negotiations.

The answer I received was, "None will work. Until the Senate has a piece of paper on the table, busy members, preoccupied with other matters, will not focus meaningfully on the issue."

The congressional involvement in diplomacy has naturally been strongest at times when the United States has been most heavily engaged abroad. At such times public concerns are most felt in the Congress. The first major congressional setback to our diplomacy was the rejection of the membership in the League of Nations in 1919.

Following World War II, the Congress, reflecting public acceptance, generally supported our greater involvement in Europe, in the United Nations, and in Asia. It was only a decade afterward, following the Korean War, the beginnings of the U.S. commitment to Vietnam, and the growing realization of the magnitude of our engagement that signs of a change began to appear.

By the mid-1950s, Congress began to resist the free use of the executive agreement (as distinguished from a treaty requiring ratification) as a basis for commitments to foreign governments. During the Eisenhower administration diplomacy was conducted as often as possible to avoid formal congressional involvement. The policy of Secretary of State John Foster Dulles to establish a band of "northern tier" states as a part of the ring of containment of the Soviet Union was primarily implemented through bilateral military assistance understandings embodied in executive agreements. The administration specifically avoided suggesting that the United States formally join the Baghdad Pact of northern tier states because this would have required Senate approval.

One of Secretary Dulles's motives in abruptly withdrawing assistance to Egypt for the Aswan Dam in 1956 was his fear that Congress might place restrictions on the freedom of executive action. The Congress had attempted to restrict aid to Yugoslavia just before the Aswan action. Dulles did not want to establish a precedent. A further attempt was made by the administration to avoid formal ratification procedures in the passage of the Middle East Resolution (the Eisenhower Doctrine) in March 1957 through a joint resolution not requiring a two-thirds vote.

Increasingly Congress feared that such actions were circumventing its authority. The efforts in the mid-1950s by Senator John Bricker of Ohio to promote legislation restricting executive agreements were beaten back, but only after a major congressional-executive fight.

The next manifestation came in the 1960s in the work of the special Senate Foreign Relations Committee in a series of hearings on U.S. commitments around the world. While specific legislation did not emerge from this series of hearings, they served as a warning to administrations not to interpret too loosely the executive power to conduct diplomacy without congressional involvement. They were a forerunner of congressional revolts that led, ultimately, to the cutting off of support for conflicts in Vietnam and Cambodia and to the War Powers Act.

The contest for authority over U.S. diplomacy between the

executive and the Congress continues. The specific issues have been aggravated by growing congressional suspicions of the good faith of administrations on matters such as the limitation on arms sales and the support for human rights. Congress reacted to what they considered a weak administration position toward the military regime in Argentina in 1977 by the Humphrey-Kennedy amendment to the Foreign Military Sales legislation prohibiting credits for arms sales to Argentina because of human rights violations.* Other, broader legislation had previously eliminated all police training abroad by the United States because of congressional concerns that such training supported undemocratic regimes.

Such congressional battles have heightened the fundamental diplomatic dilemma of how to reconcile U.S. global security interests and relations with anticommunist regimes that are either oppressive or acting contrary to our interests in some other way. Administration requests for military assistance to Pakistan, for example, have faced congressional opposition because of the human rights situation in Pakistan and the strong evidence that Pakistan has been developing a nuclear weapons facility.

The normal processes of Congress can affect our diplomatic relations, even when that is not intended. The frequent failure of Congress to pass foreign assistance legislation means that our commitments to important developing countries are either reduced or made uncertain. The failure of the Senate to confirm an ambassador to a country may be due only to sluggish procedures; but the lack of action can be seen by a foreign country as a deliberate slight.

The American public accepts the fact that Congress is involved in foreign policy and diplomacy. Americans see the congressional role as an important safeguard against diplomats who would "sell out the nation's interest." Despite this general public awareness, it is surprising how unaware the

*HR 7797, 95th Congress, 1st Session 1977.

American public appears to be of the congressional role in specific foreign policy issues. Administrations are often criticized for policies that originated in Congress and are mandated by legislation. The Carter policies on human rights, for example, were primarily reflections of congressional attitudes that had been strongly manifested during the Nixon and Ford administrations.

When assistance to Pakistan was cut off in 1979 because Islamabad failed to give the assurances required under legislation on nuclear proliferation, the executive was criticized for taking such action against a friend and ally. Little reference was made to the congressional role.

When I was under secretary, a senior official of the Department of Defense berated me for the attitude of the "State Department" in refusing to agree to military cooperation with Argentina. I pointed out that we were following the dictates of the Humphrey-Kennedy amendment. I asked whether he, as a Democrat, would wish to go to the Congress and request the repeal of that legislation. He had not been previously aware of the legislation. The issue was not raised again.

Although legislation clearly has a major impact on diplomacy, some of the more difficult problems in relations with other countries are created by open congressional hearings. In the foreign affairs field, Congress has a responsibility to conduct hearings on foreign assistance, the confirmation of officials, treaty approval, and any legislative proposals relating to the nation's foreign relations. Most hearings are public sessions. Witnesses frequently appear who are critical of the character of a foreign regime or of the personal character and conduct of a leader. Members of Congress may add their own criticism. Officials of the executive, called upon to testify, are asked to comment on the critical statements of other witnesses. The U.S. diplomat abroad must often smooth seriously ruffled sensitivities and put such hearings in perspective. The task is frequently made more difficult because the media coverage may not always attribute accurately that which is said by private citizens, by members of Congress, and by the executive witnesses. The more sensational statements make headlines abroad, sometimes with incorrect assertions that they represent official policy. The hearings that were held on U.S. policy toward the Nigerian civil war in 1968–70 were an example.

The debate over how far the United States should proceed in ignoring the opposition of the Nigerian Federal Military Government to outside assistance to the secessionist provinces of Biafra awakened strong emotions in the United States. A religious order with close ties to Massachusetts, the activity of a group of former Peace Corps volunteers who had served in the secessionist area, and the effective lobbying of representatives of Biafra created a strong pressure for relief to the Biafran area and, beyond that, for diplomatic recognition. Senator Edward Kennedy held televised hearings to dramatize the plight of Biafra. Even some administration witnesses, faced with the domestic political pressures, were lukewarm toward the Federal Military Government in Lagos. U.S. diplomats in Lagos, through the three years of that war, had to maintain satisfactory relations with Africa's largest nation in the face of strong public sentiment for Biafra in the United States and Nigerian resentment toward much that was being expressed in the congressional hearings.

There have been other examples. During the debate in 1981 on the sale of AWACS aircraft to Saudi Arabia, congressional hearings brought out sharp criticism of the Saudi regime from members and witnesses alike. Only strong efforts, both by the American Embassy in Jidda and representatives of Saudi Arabia in Washington, kept relations on an even keel.

Hearings such as those conducted by Senator Frank Church's special committee on intelligence in 1977 removed the cover on highly classified aspects of our diplomacy; testimony included many references to alleged U.S. covert activities in foreign countries. While the hearings may have had a valid domestic rationale, they served to heighten the suspicion abroad toward the activities of U.S. embassies and to further the myth of CIA involvement in areas far removed from our interests. The distinction was not always clearly made between what was proposed and what was approved in clandestine operations.

There was a time when Congress held and respected closed executive hearings. This is much less the case in recent years. If there is no leak from a closed hearing, the congressional committee demands a declassified transcript, and difficult negotiations ensue between the executive and the Congress over what shall be declassified. Diplomatic problems can be created not only by what is ultimately released but also by leaks of the details of what was deleted.

The pervasiveness of Congress in U.S. diplomatic dialogue is compounded by congressional visits abroad during which legislators conduct their own diplomacy by meeting foreign government officials and opposition leaders, by making public statements, and by visiting areas often closed to U.S. diplomats. Such visits may include members of the Senate and the House as well as staff members and investigators for the General Accounting Office, an arm of the Congress.

Congressional styles and motivations vary widely. Committee members may travel to countries and areas for which they have specific responsibility or to which specific legislation may apply. Congressmen may travel on their own, motivated by a special interest, such as narcotics in Turkey or Southeast Asia, or by constituency pressure. Some visits, like Congressman Steven Solarz's trip to North Korea in 1979, are to areas forbidden to members of the executive branch. Still others may seek to meet individuals out of bounds to executive personnel; Congressman Pete McCloskey's visit to Yasir Arafat at the height of the conflict in Beirut in 1982 is an example.

The ethnic composition of our nation has a major influence in establishing the congressional role in diplomacy.

Every congressman with constituents interested in Israel, Greece, Ireland, or South Africa feels obliged to visit the appropriate country, be seen conferring with officials, and be photographed at the right spots. Countries with such ethnic links are aware of the power they have over the conduct of U.S. diplomacy on any matter of vital interest to them. To the members of Congress, it seems perfectly natural to regard Jerusalem, Athens, Dublin, or Pretoria as a further extension of the congressional district.

American diplomats have been patient and discreet over the years about the operational problems of hosting members of Congress overseas. While most are serious travelers, a few clearly seem to believe that once they leave the shores of the United States they are no longer bound by the rules of conduct that presumably guided them in their own districts. Their shopping, entertaining, sometimes lavish use of foreign currency, uncertain schedules, statements and photographs for domestic consumption, and demands of protocol are accepted as part of the diplomat's job. Foreign service officers have learned to cope with and make amends for occasional bizarre behavior and discourteous remarks.

The impact of congressional visits on U.S. official diplomacy is largely determined by the degree to which the visitors support official policy in their actions and statements. The programs of congressional delegations are generally arranged by members of the U.S. embassy, and individuals may stay in embassy residences. Not surprisingly, local officials and the public in many countries see these visitors as "official" and are puzzled by any comments that depart from known U.S. policies and attitudes. Most members, even if opposed to an administration, realize that they are Americans abroad and mute their criticism of official policy, but a few will purposely seek a foreign setting to denounce U.S. actions.

U.S. domestic politics and the reflection of Washington political struggles are never far below the surface of congressional visits abroad. The member of Congress comes from a culture that encourages free, provocative, and, at times, irresponsible speech. When abroad, the politician concentrates primarily on the audience at home. Public statements by members of Congress when overseas, therefore, may at times include candid comments on a foreign scene that are popular with the constituents back home but stir up a diplomatic storm abroad.

Members of Congress seeking to show their distance from administration support of authoritarian regimes will ask embassies to arrange meetings with dissidents and opposition leaders. In some countries, even though some political risk to the embassy may be present, help in arranging such visits can convey locally a positive signal that, despite official policy, the embassy is aware of the presence of other voices in the country.

Members of the Senate Foreign Relations Committee will normally work closely with American embassies, and the ambassador may join most, if not all, of their meetings with local officials. Those from other committees may prefer to act on their own, often directly setting up their own appointments even before arrival; embassies may not even know of such arrangements or be briefed on private meetings.

From time to time, members of Congress will visit countries they have attacked on the floor of Congress. The ambassador, in conversations with foreign leaders, may have pointed to such congressional opposition as an example of problems created by the actions or policies of the foreign government. The ambassador will urge the congressman or senator, in meetings with officials in that country, to repeat the criticism. Frequently, the member of Congress will say, "Oh, that's your job to give the bad news. We are here to be friendly." A polite and meaningless meeting ensues; afterward the local leader may ask the ambassador, "What did you mean when you said this congressman was critical of our policies? He didn't say anything to me." In such fashion is diplomatic credibility destroyed.

Congressional visitors will on occasion try to use trips abroad to gain ammunition with which to attack administration policy at home, either by eliciting statements from a U.S. official or seeking documents that have been denied by the executive branch in Washington. Nearly every American diplomat has encountered the breezy congressman who says, "Now, Mr. Ambassador, I assume you see things somewhat differently from Washington. Tell me, off the record, what is your own view of this policy?" Nearly every diplomat has also learned that, for some members of Congress, "off the record" is a meaningless term. Except in rare instances, there cannot be a fully frank exchange between diplomats and members of Congress and their staffs on policy issues.

At times, members of Congress have learned of reports from embassies that may take issue with a Washington assessment. When a request to the executive branch for the report has been refused, visitors may seek the report from embassies abroad. U.S. diplomats also learn to be cautious in any sharing of documents with congressional visitors without approval from the Department of State.

Although such visits may occasionally puzzle foreign officials and embarrass U.S. diplomats, on balance they represent a positive extension of U.S. diplomacy abroad. Most members are responsible officials, sharing in the distaste for the poor judgment of some of their colleagues. Congressional visits often help to open doors to American diplomats and provide occasions to see officials who may not be otherwise readily accessible, particularly military officials. Relationships can be established that can be further nurtured after the members of Congress have departed. The role of congressional members both in highlighting the situation in the Philippines in 1986 and in observing the election had a major and positive influence on the course of events.

Diplomats and policymakers feel differently about cases in which individual members of Congress, whether at home or abroad, have involved themselves, often with damaging results, directly in the diplomatic process. Two such cases were the fall of Somoza in Nicaragua and the incident of the Soviet brigade in Cuba.

In 1979 in Nicaragua it seemed clear that the dictator of that country, Anastasio Somoza, could survive, if at all, only with substantial repression and outside help. His policies of expanding his family holdings and suppressing the opposition, particularly after the earthquake of 1974, had created overwhelming opposition. In the absence of a moderate center, the likelihood was that the more radical Sandinistas, supported by Cuba, might come to power. Neighboring Central American states, as well as the United States, wanted neither civil war nor a Sandinista takeover. Under the umbrella of the Organization of American States, a tripartite commission was formed to mediate a transition of power to a moderate alternative. The United States, Guatemala, and the Dominican Republic were members.

Congressman John Murphy of Staten Island had been a roommate of Somoza in prep school and a colleague at West Point. He strongly supported Somoza's desire to remain in power. Throughout the mediation the two conferred nightly by telephone. Murphy urged him not to agree to step down; he used his position in the Congress to lobby on Somoza's behalf in Washington. Perhaps the mediation had few prospects for success, but the intervention of a U.S. congressman in a delicate diplomatic process did not help the achievement of a moderate outcome to the crisis in Nicaragua.

In the summer of 1979, the United States was involved diplomatically in a number of critical issues in Central America and with the Soviet Union. The SALT II treaty was before the Senate. Havana was about to host the meeting of non-aligned states, and the United States was seeking quietly to blunt Cuban efforts further to radicalize that movement.

At that point Senator Richard Stone of Florida, who, by virtue of a large Cuban exile population in his district, paid attention to developments in Cuba and had his own sources of information, learned of the possible presence of a Soviet combat brigade near Havana. The administration confirmed the leaked information to Stone and felt obliged, at the same time, to inform the chairman of the Senate Foreign Relations Committee, Senator Frank Church. Senator Church, having once before been stung politically in a matter involving Cuba, made public demands on the administration to seek the removal of the brigade. The pressures of the congressional inquiries and statements resulted in a crisis that affected the U.S. ability to deal with several of the issues on the diplomatic agenda. There is little doubt that the incident further reduced the Senate support for the SALT II treaty. The tragedy was that the congressional intervention and the public pressures provided little opportunity and time to determine the facts: the brigade had been there since 1962.*

Generally the relationship of the American diplomat to members of Congress is a passive one. The effort is designed to assist members and to minimize the confusion that may be created by their criticism of official policy.

The different missions and perspectives of the diplomat and the member of Congress mean that the relationship will never be a completely easy one. The ambassador or the embassy officer is clearly working for the administration in power. Friendship with members of Congress may go back into previous administrations; those members will expect the diplomat to display an honest candor about events regardless of the administration in power. Committees that call embassy officials as witnesses may expect that State Department personnel will present the official policy; they look to the embassy official to share the assessment on the ground as he or she sees it. The capacity to maintain credibility in dealings with members of Congress without, at times, risking conspicuous criticism of the policies of an administration can test the

---

*David D. Newsom, *The Soviet Brigade in Cuba: A Study in Political Diplomacy* (Bloomington: Indiana University Press, 1987).

skill of an American diplomat more severely than most encounters with a foreign government.

More and more in recent years senior members of the diplomatic service have become active lobbyists for policies in the Congress. Where a specific aid project or a particular negotiation is in trouble in the Congress, the American ambassador and sometimes officers of the embassy are brought back to persuade members of Congress to vote for or against specific legislation.

Congressional reform and the dilution of responsibility in the Senate and House have made the process of consultation with the Congress on diplomatic issues infinitely more complicated. The ambassador home on leave or the State Department official could, two decades ago, get a sense of what Congress might do and influence the direction of action by speaking with a few key committee chairmen and minority members. That is no longer the case. Committees outside those formally charged with foreign affairs, such as Armed Services, Judiciary, and Foreign Commerce, play a substantial role, largely unchecked by leadership authority. Those committees that have primarily a domestic responsibility are less willing to be influenced by the nation's diplomatic problems. A single member pursuing a special preoccupation can frustrate broader diplomatic designs.

In the American system, Congress is by law, tradition, and politics a significant factor in the conduct of the diplomacy of the United States. Although it is in the interests of both diplomatic and political cultures to find better ways to work together to preserve and advance the interests of the nation, the differences between the cultures are inherent in our constitution and inescapable in practice. Effective U.S. diplomacy is by no means rendered impossible by this division, but the task of explaining the U.S. system to foreign officials and working within it effectively to negotiate and persuade will always present diplomatic problems unique to this country.

V

⌒

DIPLOMACY AND THE MEDIA

IN ANY COUNTRY, diplomacy and the press are uneasy adversaries. The diplomat believes the less said the better. The press thrives on public utterances. Nowhere is this relationship freer of official restraints than in the United States; even other democracies place limitations on the full exercise of press freedom. A French journalist once remarked to an audience in Washington, "The American media not only has no constraints, but its economic power is such that it can cover a story in such totality that its impact is far greater than the capacity of countries with less resources."

The influence of this free institution on diplomacy is twofold. It forms the crucible in which policy issues are shaped in the nation. It disseminates information and images of the United States abroad—at times in conflict with official diplomacy.

The media, including both the print press and television, are significant actors in the diplomatic arena of the U.S. democracy. In Washington, government and press must live side by side; decisions in foreign policy are made on a public stage. This is not a situation to be deplored or resented; it is one to be accepted as a part of the freedom that underlies American democracy.

The media role in foreign affairs has been dramatically enhanced by television. Television, following the concept of news that has always dominated the media, is looking for that which is unusual, dramatic, graphic. The impact of pictures of violence coming into a living room is far greater than a description of a similar event in the cold, black type of a newspaper. This development has raised serious questions, each one a matter of continuing debate. Has it made the Americans, as a people, less ready to be involved in situations that threaten conflict? Do television cameras in an area of disturbance tempt demonstrators to riot for the camera, conveying an inaccurate impression of the state and nature of the disturbance?

No clear answers to these questions have emerged from the extensive arguments between those in the TV world and those concerned with its impact. What is agreed is that, today, the majority of Americans receive most of their news about foreign affairs from television. Participants and viewers alike will probably also agree that television, by its very nature, gives a superficial view of complicated events. During German elections some years ago, an American television network assigned a top reporter and camera crew to prepare a ten minute news spot on the elections. The reporter and crew spent three weeks in Germany in preparation. Because of the pressure of other news, when the film was finally aired the producer required that it be cut to only one and three-quarters minutes. This sort of thing no doubt occurs regularly.

Television is superficial, but it is stark and intrusive, sometimes to a degree deeply resented by those it pursues. In 1979, I went to Germany to receive the first thirteen of the Iranian hostages who were released. We set up telephone booths for them to call their families from the military hospital in Weisbaden. I recall one of the hostages emerging from a booth, red with anger and near to tears. He said, "I called my

family to hear how they were and to tell them I was all right. All I got was a diatribe from my mother about how they had been bothered by the television crews camping night and day on their lawn."

For both television and the print media, the most serious question in relations with the government involves the coverage of matters affecting national security. This was at the heart of the controversy over the exclusion of the media from the Grenada invasion in 1983 and surfaced again in discussions of the reaction of the media to the TWA hijacking in Athens in 1985. To what extent should the press and television of the United States take into account the national interest or considerations of sensitive diplomatic negotiations in crisis situations? There is no doubt that premature disclosure by the media of military actions can cost lives and, possibly, even the success of the action. Neither is there any doubt that the presence of cameras can give terrorists what they want: publicity for their cause. Those who support the freedom of the media to decide such issues can point to the failure of the press to disclose the Bay of Pigs project as an example of media restraint that contributed to a disaster. They can also argue that the presence of cameras in hostage situations saves lives by making the killing of the hostages less likely.

U.S. media representatives have heeded requests from U.S. officials not to publish items, but, almost always, in cases in which reporters and editors were convinced that U.S. lives were at stake. But it is the press—and not the government—that makes the final decisions.

Representatives of the media resist suggestions that they play an influential role in the diplomatic process. To preserve their credibility as news gatherers, they want to be seen only as observers. But, from the perspective of someone in government, their influence is much greater than that of a mere observer. U.S. newspapers, wire services, news magazines, and television networks, with their substantial resources and their dynamic initiative provide to the American people a

window on the world. The news seen through that window influences the development and implementation of policy.

Today the flow of news is more rapid than ever. The flood of information stimulates and prods the making and implementation of foreign policy. United States diplomacy is frequently "catching up." Public perceptions of events are created before officials have a chance to shape the perception or to correct misapprehensions. In a day when television communication, in particular, is instantaneous, news of fast breaking events in some foreign country reaches American homes well before information comes to Washington from U.S. representatives overseas. The fast breaking news creates immediate pressures on the government for statements, even before embassies have had an opportunity to inform the Department of State and other agencies. When Anwar Sadat, the president of Egypt, was assassinated, the U.S. government was seeking formal verification of his death long after the wire services and television had concluded that Sadat had died. The State Department was criticized for this delay, but to have made such an announcement before the formal statement of the Egyptian government had been issued would have been a serious diplomatic offence.

The diplomat cannot become a news reporter. A correct official account of an event requires that facts be checked, the local government be consulted, and recommendations for action be prepared. Often this must be done during a crisis, when the normally lethargic systems of some countries are slowed even more.

The focal points of the U.S. government-media relationship are the daily briefings. Every day, in the White House, the Department of Defense, and the Department of State, an official spokesperson meets with more than a hundred foreign and domestic representatives of the press, wire services, news magazines, and television. Briefings are periodically supplemented by press conferences with the president and secretary of state. These performances are on camera. The diplomat abroad is conscious that, whatever official instructions may say on a key issue, those instructions can be suddenly altered in the give and take of a noon briefing or a high-level press conference.

The secretary of state's morning is likely to begin with a meeting with the department's press officer and an effort to identify those stories of the day that may bring questions. The secretary will look for those cables from embassies abroad that will help or possibly specifically recommend what should be said in response to anticipated questions. If the decision is made to say nothing, it is made with the recognition that silence cannot continue for more than two or three days.

The time has passed when departmental press officers have the luxury of refusing to answer a question. In times of crisis, the lack of response can lead to politically embarrassing charges of uncertainty, vacillation, lack of policy, or "cover-up." Although it would occasionally be wiser diplomatically for the United States to avoid answering questions officially, the daily briefings and the close access that reporters have to senior officials in the State Department and the White House make it inevitable that questions will be posed. In an atmosphere often charged with suspicion of government motives, refusal to answer is not a way out. "No comment" is no longer an acceptable response.

When the government does reply and makes a statement, that statement becomes part of an official public exchange with other countries. The U.S. words are studied in foreign offices and for their significance. Both friends and adversaries of the United States may feel obliged to comment. During the Iranian hostage crisis, when there was no official contact between Iran and the United States, statements to the press and on radio and television took the place of official communications.

The media also puts pressure on diplomacy through the Congress. The general reaction of executive branch officials to a policy suggestion in the press is defensive. Seldom is it, "This looks good, let's study it." The approach is more likely to be, "How do we turn off this one?" Let a member of an important committee of Congress telephone and ask about the idea and the likelihood is that it will be seriously studied. Those who have been witnesses before congressional committees know, also, that the front page of the *New York Times* or the *Washington Post* or the morning television news are more likely to set the agenda and establish the questions for a hearing than the carefully prepared papers of the staff or the executive.

In the United States, the media is, as it should be, a forum for debate on international issues and on U.S. policies. Not only domestic issues but also the concerns and conflicts of other countries are debated in the U.S. press and television. Proponents of different sides in internal conflicts such as those in Central America or Africa will seek to reach the American public and, through the public, the Congress. The American public becomes the judge and jury of other people's quarrels. The verdict is rendered by executive policies and by votes in the Congress on such matters as foreign assistance and arms sales.

These debates can have a major influence on diplomacy by shaping the public perceptions of an issue. Nicaragua becomes not just a Central American issue, but an East-West issue. The debates are often set off by leaks of information to the press that upset the timetable of orderly diplomacy.

In Washington, leaks are no longer a plumbing problem, they are a political and diplomatic problem. One can identify five types of leaks: the "ego" leak by the person who wants to demonstrate how much he or she knows; the advocacy leak by someone who wants to promote a policy; or, the reverse, the dissent leak by someone who feels open debate will sabotage a policy. A fourth is the calculated leak by those at the top who want either to send up a trial balloon or to reveal a decision in something less than an official way.

There is a fifth kind of sudden revelation that is not a true leak. A smart Washington reporter can spot black limousines entering the southwest gate of the White House on a Sunday afternoon and, by determining who is in the cars, can guess with remarkable accuracy the reason for the meeting and possibly even its agenda. By phone calls to unsuspecting people in the bureaucracy, the reporter can often develop a story that may be characterized as a leak by unhappy officials. The best of the Washington reporters have been around longer than most officials and know which buttons to press.

The leak can be especially damaging in matters that involve governments other than the United States: the revelation of a U.S. negotiating position; the disclosure of information given in confidence by a foreign official; or the premature discussion of an issue still under closed debate in a foreign capital. Such information can seriously embarrass negotiators and lessen the confidence others may have in sharing secrets with U.S. diplomats.

Leaks can backfire. I was told that the official who leaked the story of the mining of the Nicaraguan harbors by the CIA in 1984 did so believing knowledge of these actions would increase public support for administration policies. The leak, arousing domestic and world opinion against the action, had the opposite effect.

Whatever the nature of the leak, the phenomenon adds to the natural caution of the diplomat. Phrases that may attract the attention of a potential leaker or assessments or recommendations that could cause embarrassment to either government are avoided or toned down in messages to Washington. As a young officer I was once advised, "Never write a telegram you would be unwilling to see on the front page of the *Washington Post*." Diplomats are not fond of stories that say, "While the government obviously intends to continue with its policy in ———, it is known that the Ambassador in ——— has strongly recommended against this course of action."

While the presence of media representatives in Washington creates pressures on the government to make foreign policy decisions, the presence of reporters abroad can, in some measure, determine the issues that must be addressed. News, at times, is where the media representatives happen to be. If there is a crisis in Central America and the newspapers and television networks are sending the bulk of their correspondents and crews to that area, that will be at the top of the foreign policy agenda. The resultant coverage will create the questions, the congressional hearings, and the public concern that will force the U.S. government to comment or respond through action.

Even more pressure for official comment is sometimes generated by the individual initiative of a journalist. The revelation in the press of a scandal or weakness in a strong U.S. ally can cast doubt on the underlying assumptions of a policy. Congressional pressures may require a review of a policy, even if the administration is not inclined to do so. Stories of the excesses of the Marcos regime spurred investigations in the House of Representatives that were a factor in the ultimate shift of U.S. support to Marcos's opponents.

Journalists from time to time seek out individuals who are unavailable to diplomats, either because of official policy, the sensitivity of local governments, or remoteness. These might be officials of the Palestine Liberation Organization or guerrilla leaders in Central America. The reporter who is interviewing such a person is conducting diplomacy. That public account will shape views toward the movement and toward official policy. Although the government may have other means of evaluating the strength and nature of a movement, the public reactions to such interviews may place limits on official action; conversely, a poor portrayal of a radical leader may strengthen U.S. policies in support of the existing government. Individuals such as Yasir Arafat and Fidel Castro use their interview opportunities to speak both to the government and to the American public through the media.

While the news and views brought by the media serve to influence the making of policy in Washington, the actions of the press and television also have a direct impact on the work of the American diplomat in the field. U.S. foreign service officers must at times explain the nature of the free press to foreigners bewildered by different versions of a policy, seek to quiet angry reactions to media stories about a foreign country, and establish an effective working relationship with both local journalists and those representing U.S. media services abroad.

Each morning, around the world, diplomats of the United States pick up the daily Wireless File—several pages of news and opinion transmitted by the USIA. The file contains official statements and speeches as well as a summary of the daily press and television news at home, often marked "not for distribution." To the diplomat, the latter is as important as the government texts. For what the press says is also part of the total message of the United States to the rest of the world. The diplomat must have both messages in mind when approaching a foreign government.

"I appreciate that that is your official position," the foreign ministry official may say after a formal presentation by an American diplomat. That official may, at the same time, be saying to himself, or openly, "But how do you reconcile that with the *New York Times* report yesterday morning that the National Security Council staff is making a different recommendation to the president?"

So deeply ingrained in many countries is the concept of a controlled press that it is difficult for an American diplomat to explain the free expression in the United States. In countries where the press is essentially a government organ—and this represents a majority of the countries in the world—the less sophisticated official will insist that criticism of his or her country in the U.S. press is officially inspired. In the many lands where the conspiracy theory of history prevails, officials look for the dark reason behind the fact that the U.S. diplomat may be speaking in friendly terms while the press of the United States is taking quite a different line.

I was once confronted by a Saudi Arabian diplomat complaining about a story in the *New York Times* on his country. I explained that the *Times* was an independent newspaper and that if the United States government were to lodge a protest with the *Times* over the story it would probably only bring more adverse stories. The Saudi replied, "You cannot tell me that you have a free press in the United States. Every day at noon you call in all the reporters to the State Department and tell them what to print about foreign policy." I arranged for the diplomat to attend a noon briefing, with its active give and take. I never felt that the experience persuaded him; it was too far from the concept of the press with which he was familiar.

The assumption that the press somehow represents an official position frequently means that comments in the American press considered insulting or unfriendly develop into diplomatic issues. In 1948, two key figures in the politics of the Indo-Pakistan subcontinent died: Mahatma Gandhi and Mohammad Ali Jinnah. The treatment in the U.S. press of the two figures was sharply contrasting. Gandhi was seen as a peacemaker, a quasi-saint, a martyr. Jinnah was depicted as a stern, unyielding man, who was partly responsible for the sub-continent's troubles. Those of us conducting official business in Pakistan during that period faced the public anger and the diplomatic protests of the Pakistanis over the portrayal in the U.S. press of the life and death of the nation's founder.

To the diplomat, observing the U.S. press through the eyes of others, the coverage of world events shows a stark lack of sensitivity to the feelings and interests of non-Americans. The U.S.-centered focus may be natural, yet it is seen abroad as accentuating the lack of genuine interest in the United States in the fates and problems of others. In the news of any major disaster, the emphasis is always on how many Americans were killed or injured. Particularly galling to foreigners is the domestic U.S. coverage of official visits by foreigners to Washington. If there is television coverage it is likely to focus on the

U.S. president; the foreign visitor may be seen only inciden- tally, as a backdrop to the give and take between the president and reporters on issues totally unrelated to the visit.

To some extent American diplomats abroad can influence how a nation is presented in the U.S. press by their rela- tionships with journalists at the post. Each U.S. diplomat must make decisions with respect to relations with the media. Much depends on experience and inclination. The person who has dealt frequently with the press at home and feels at ease with journalists will follow that practice abroad. There are different approaches depending on whether one is dealing with the press of the country or with representatives of the U.S. press. In many countries, the local press representatives come from party newspapers with varying points of view, often philosophically unfriendly to the United States. An American ambassador has difficulty in getting a fair hearing in such organs.

The relationship between U.S. diplomats and U.S. press representatives abroad will vary. The locally based American correspondents, who have a stake in maintaining good rela- tions with all elements in a country, are generally cooperative with both U.S. embassy personnel and local officials. There have been many instances of U.S. ambassadors sitting down frequently with such representatives for off the record ex- changes. Each group has much to learn from the other, par- ticularly in countries where access is limited. Llewelyn Thompson, one of the great U.S. diplomats, used to hold weekly "seminars" with correspondents in Moscow at which each shared views candidly.

Mirroring a situation in Washington, even relations with American correspondents abroad have become more difficult in the post-Watergate, post-Vietnam era when a more con- frontational atmosphere was created between press and gov- ernment. Whatever the inclination of the local diplomat and correspondent, the pressure for "disclosures" from editors at home can frustrate any genuine dialogue.

Reporters have different views regarding their relationship to a U.S. embassy abroad or to the government at home. Some recognize a national interest and may share impressions and information they do not put into their stories. Others feel that any contact with U.S. officials will jeopardize their future access as a reporter.

U.S. diplomats must always be conscious that what they report in official channels may be reported back to the country in the press and that they may be seen as the source. This is often true in circumstances in which press reporters are barred from a country in a time of crisis. The only word the United States may be receiving is from its embassy in that country. When the State Department or some other Washington source reports publicly information that comes from the embassy, even if the source is not given, the foreign government will presume that the embassy is the source. In such cases, important sources of information may dry up.

In the day of rapid communication and the necessity to encourage positive public support for policies, U.S. diplomats sometimes become media personalities. The U.S. ambassador to El Salvador, for example, was on the morning talk shows for several days in a row just before elections in that country in 1984.

Whatever the personal relationship, diplomats will always feel a sense of caution in dealing with the press, whether in Washington or abroad. The American press and public often question the insistence on anonymity by U.S. officials when providing information. The official may insist that story may be attributed to "a Western diplomatic official" or "a government source." This is done to protect an embassy in such circumstances. It is a also part of a diplomatic convention that dilutes the official nature of a statement if the actual source is not given. The pressure is less, in such cases, to reply if it is not clearly "an official statement."

Diplomats are always conscious that they are never speaking to just one audience. Whatever is said is likely to reach beyond the immediate environment; when that is deliberately or accidentally distorted, diplomats must move quickly to be certain that the correct version is in the public domain.

Whether in Washington or in foreign countries, press disclosures have no doubt upset the careful planning of foreign policies. But, if we look at the question of whether the media are friends or foes of effective diplomacy, we need to look at two other questions: the power of the government and the importance of freedom.

Although the press and television have great power in the United States, in the last analysis it is the executive that has the power to dominate the news, particularly when the government is led by a competent communicator. As long as statements of the president and key members of the cabinet are news, these officials will have the capacity to exercise strong influence on public perceptions. Those in the executive can determine when they will or will not appear on television talk shows or give interviews, and the timing and nature of press conferences. Speeches on major international issues by high officials can also dominate the front page and the evening news. The time and place of all these events are largely in the hands of the government leadership.

There will never be agreement between the government sector and the media on the boundaries of press involvement in diplomacy. The question will continue to be debated whether a democracy such as that in the United States can be effective in its international relations and preserve totally its freedoms to speak, to write, and to print. But it is more disturbing to conclude that we can only be more effective in the world if we curb not only what we, but others who look at us, regard as our most precious heritage.

In the midst of the TWA hostage crisis in 1985, London's *Economist*, addressing this question, commented, "This is how a free society is made to pay for its freedom: internal freedom to know is enhanced at the cost of external freedom to act." That is the dilemma of every democracy.

V I

⚓

THE PRESSURE FOR
INFORMATION

INFORMATION IS THE LIFE blood of diplomacy. Whether the process of gathering information is characterized as reporting or espionage, the success of a diplomatic mission depends heavily on its ability to keep Washington well and accurately informed both of present events and likely future developments. The search for information, in turn, encounters political and cultural resistance abroad that, in some societies, adversely affects the image others have of the United States and its diplomatic pursuits.

Driven by global responsibilities, fear of surprises, and an innate curiosity, the American appetite for information is insatiable. Under the challenges of the instantaneous reporting of TV, the analyses of the press, and the public's knowledge of global events, the U.S. diplomat is expected to report not only what is but also what can be expected. Government analysts dissect the information critically, minutely, and often publicly.

It is little wonder that many in sensitive societies regard the United States as excessively intrusive. Americans' questions can awaken suspicions even in friendly countries. The demands of the diplomacy of a free society inevitably clash with the sensitivities of a majority of the nations of the world where questions are less common and less tolerated.

The hunger for information has resulted in a vast increase in the flow of messages to Washington. In the 35 years between 1947 and 1982, telegraphic traffic to the Department of State from diplomatic posts increased 5 times, a result of the greater global involvement of the United States, an increase in the number of diplomatic posts, and the rapid acceleration of the business of diplomacy.

In prewar years the telegram was used only for urgent or particularly important matters. The diplomatic pouch, carried by couriers, was the channel for most reporting. The pouch has since become largely the medium for long-term instructions, "think pieces," and administrative traffic. Despite frequent requests from Washington to cut back on telegrams, U.S. diplomats abroad came to realize that, in today's world, only the telegram commanded attention.

Curiously, the greater urgency and volume of information has meant greater restrictions on its use in decision making and diplomacy. In a capital where information is power, a constant struggle goes on between those who attempt to limit the distribution of information to those who "need to know" and those who, out of asserted operational need, pride, or curiosity, dispute the restriction. The originator in a diplomatic mission can suggest how the message is to be restricted; the Secretariat in the Department of State, however, will be the final arbiter.

Who generates the appetite for diplomatic information? Ambassadors and their staffs at a mission can, of course, initiate information out of a sense of what Washington may require, to warn of coming events, or to remind Washington of their presence and activity.

The U.S. diplomat is aware, when specific requests are made, of the many demanding users in the executive complex. The secretary of state and his immediate staff need to be on top of developments in the most significant and critical areas of the world. Officers in the bureaus and desks below the secretary must be prepared to respond to queries or to initiate action in those areas not in the immediate spotlight. The National Security Council staff, increasingly influential in policy making, demands the latest on those issues in the forefront of the news or in which the president is involved. Other parts of the White House, such as the Office of Management and Budget, insist that they, too, must be aware of immediate and sensitive developments in foreign affairs. The Department of Defense, a strong player in the field of foreign policy, has its own apparatus that must be fed with the daily gleanings from abroad. The Joint Chiefs of Staff and the respective service organizations are participants in the policy deliberations; they, too, need to know. The intelligence community, led by the CIA, has heavy responsibilities to analyze as well as to collect. The USIA and the Agency for International Development are important overseas actors. Their officials, too, want to be fully informed. Other departments, such as Treasury, Commerce, and Agriculture have their special interests abroad, and they need to know not only what affects their particular interests but also the broader international background against which their interests must be viewed.

Except for the National Security Council, each of these bureaucratic players in Washington has its representatives in embassies abroad. Although the ambassador is responsible for coordinating the work of the mission, including the reporting, each agency representative, in fact, has the capacity to report directly through "back channel" messages to their counterparts in Washington.

What are the pressures that generate this thirst for information? Pressure begins with the fact that foreign policy is near the top of every administration's agenda. The United States is heavily involved throughout the world. When dramatic news reaches the desks of foreign affairs agencies in

Washington, pressure is immediately generated by senior officials for some kind of official response. Usually more information is required, and urgent messages go out that request
further probing by the posts abroad.

American diplomats are also conscious of the information
requirements of the daily noon press briefings when the
spokespersons must respond to questions on the primary
issues of the day. For such occasions and for presidential and
secretarial news conferences, the appearance of being as informed as the media and the ability to be able to answer the
toughest questions are indispensable to political success. The
press will not wait long for official word before framing its
own conclusions.

Information is the raw material for making difficult decisions on crises and for establishing the U.S. positions in negotiations. In crisis situations, policy pressures lead to the
creation of "task forces" that operate around the clock, following events and supporting those dealing with the issues in the
field. Such task forces have a constant need for information to
answer questions from higher officials, to provide the raw
material for instructions, and to deal with the press and the
public. Their pressures are symbolized by lights burning
through the night in the State Department and embassies
abroad.

To avoid surprises—unacceptable to most leaders of
strong nations—information from diplomatic missions is
needed to feed the demand for analysis, for estimates of the
stability of friendly regimes, for predictions of what may
happen in countries or regions of importance to the United
States. Such information is the life blood of the batteries of
experts in the Department of State, the Pentagon, and the
CIA.

Congress generates a part of the demand for information.
During a tour in the embassy in London, I was struck by how
modest were the requirements for information placed upon

the British Foreign Office by the Parliament. Because of the parliamentary system and strong party control, the Foreign Office was largely the arbiter of what would or would not be given to the Parliament. It is not that way in the United States.

Congress, in its authorization of programs and its appropriation of foreign affairs funds, requires substantial amounts of information. More and more, in the conduct of their daily business, the leading committees responsible for foreign and defense affairs—and their staff members—wish to be informed of the details of international developments. The Top Secret *National Intelligence Digest* is shared with key congressional committees. By their further queries, as well as by the demands of legislation, they add to the pressures on U.S. diplomacy for information. Where Congress itself may not generate such pressure, watchdog offices, responsible for congressional relations in the State Department, Defense Department, and the White House, will do so.

Pressures are generated not only by congressional requirements, but also by the frequent debates over policies and programs that take place within the executive. The problem is especially acute where sharp differences exist, either over an approach to a sensitive issue, such as the Middle East, or over the nature and level of an aid program. Partisans on both sides will use reports from the field to argue their case. Some will immediately request additional or balancing information from embassies to bolster their arguments. Assessments from the field that suggest political weaknesses in an aid recipient can tempt budget cutters and rival claimants at home to demand that funds be withdrawn from the nation in trouble. Reports of economic weakness or project mismanagement can generate similar requests. Candid reporting can result in substantial cuts in an assistance program. An ambassador in Tunisia carefully crafted his reports to insure that there would be no ammunition in Washington for those who might want to take aid funds away. One can argue that in the interests of long-term relations with an important North African country he was right to do so.

Around the world, in 135 embassies and 98 consulates-general and consulates, ambassadors and officers feel these pressures for information. How do they meet the demand? In the United States, information is relatively easy to obtain. Although Americans may react negatively at times to the foreigner who seems too curious or too prying, the general assumption is that everyone should be open and forthcoming. When they are not, they are accused of being stubborn, or of "covering up." This is not the case in most other societies— even in other democracies. No one presumes that information should be shared, even with friendly foreign, including American, diplomats.

Open and official sources are available in virtually every country. The right of an embassy officer to pose questions in the foreign ministry is accepted, even if answers may not be given. Newspapers, radio, and television provide some news in nearly every country. In many, however, the media is government owned and information is limited to official releases.

Even in countries where the sharing of information may not be inhibited, the problem may be to obtain or confirm information rapidly. Office hours of officials abroad are, in most cases, limited. If the telephone system works, officials and individuals may be reluctant to use it, either because it is not customary to do so or because others may be listening in. The dense traffic of some foreign cities may require three hours or more for the round trip from the embassy to a government office. In a time of crisis three hours can be a long time.

In few countries are there established methods of briefing the press or foreign missions. Diplomatic missions in Washington benefit from the instant replay of departmental press briefings and from the fact that correspondents from their countries are accredited to the White House and the Departments of State and Defense. These correspondents can share not only the information but also the background and atmosphere of a discussion. In very few countries do U.S. correspondents have comparable access to government sources. Where such access does exist, American journalists may be reluctant to share this information with the embassy.

The language ability of embassy personnel abroad is also important in gaining information. Although many foreign officials speak English, some of the most important individuals may not. Language becomes important in establishing the unofficial relationships that are often the key to an understanding of a society. Speaking informally with a foreign official after a formal session has ended or seizing an opportunity at a dinner or reception to talk with someone from the official circle can only be accomplished with an adequate knowledge of the language of the country. Similarly, U.S. diplomats are well ahead if they can at least scan a local newspaper and quickly digest the radio or television news.

Breaking through into another society takes time. The U.S. diplomat is usually in a country no more than three or four years; most feel it takes at least a year to reach a basic familiarity with a new country. The Westernized "jet set" are always ready to welcome the American, but they scarcely represent the opinion of a nation. The most difficult task for an American diplomat seeking information in a foreign environment is to break out of the normal circle of diplomatic contacts to meet and talk with people of different strata of society and often of different points of view.

In many societies, diplomats encounter unexpected barriers in seeking broader access to the people of the country. In some capitals, the Foreign Ministry requires that all invitations to local people be transmitted through the government. Those who may be entertained in the relative luxury of an American embassy believe they cannot, without embarrassment, return the favor in their own modest homes. Others, for political reasons, may be wary; they may not wish to be seen

or identified with a foreign embassy officer. Language, sensitivity, and reduced ostentation can, to some extent, break
through such barriers. Moving beyond the official, cultural,
and social restrictions is more than an exercise in social
contact or in understanding a society. It is essential if an
American diplomat is to give to Washington an accurate analysis of that country's future.

Acquiring the information that Washington needs means
building, with the participation of all embassy officers, a
wide network that includes officials, businessmen, journalists, economists, professors, and ordinary people in the
capital city and elsewhere in the country. The diplomat who
remains in the capital will often miss trends and attitudes
outside the capital essential to a full understanding of a country's condition.

There are other sources, as well. The American community
in a country can provide a deep understanding of the country,
although long residence, sensitivity, and objectivity do not
always go together. Other diplomatic missions may also have
associations and insights that complement those of the American embassy.

Building and maintaining a network is difficult, even in
friendly countries. In most developing countries, restrictions
exist on the travel of diplomats. The reason, often given and
often legitimate, is that adequate facilities for accommoda-
tion and travel can be provided only by the government.
Notice must be given and permission requested. In some
authoritarian societies, diplomatic social invitations must be
distributed through the foreign ministry where, of course, the
guest lists are reviewed. Security services follow the contacts
of embassy officers; more than once an ambassador has been
reminded that junior officers are meeting with persons or
organizations considered by the local government to be inap-
propriate.

The style of acquiring information is important. The most
effective diplomats will be discreet as they seek or acquire

information. Conversations will flow easily into areas of comfortable interest to the foreigner. Such dialogue, if effective, will also give to the foreigner the feeling that questions can be avoided without embarrassment. The kind of direct questioning of strangers that is common in American society is uncommon elsewhere. The diplomat who has stored up a series of questions before attending a social function is much less effective. As he moves from guest to guest, the questions are posed in order. The other guests are clearly aware that he is writing a report.

In one of my posts, an Asian ambassador would approach me regularly at evening receptions just after listening to the BBC news. One by one he would bring up the items on the news and ask my opinion. If the reception was on a Thursday evening, the questions would be more detailed. I knew that he was going to spend the evening writing a despatch for his weekly diplomatic bag.

The aggressive seeking of information abroad must always be weighed against other factors. To what extent will the source be placed in jeopardy by a visit or a telephone call? To what extent will the information acquired, if it leaks in Washington, be traced to a local source to the peril of that source? To what extent will seeking this information create resistance, "use up currency" that may make it difficult to go back to the source on an even more significant matter? The quest for knowledge must always be balanced against the security of the source and future access.

With the strong pressure for information and with the variety of overt and covert sources tapped by most embassies, the task of the ambassador becomes one of evaluating what is obtained. At times, foreign sources will give different stories to different officers of the embassy. The task of assessment is rendered even more complicated by the practice of separate reporting to Washington by various agencies represented abroad, including the CIA. Separate reports can sometimes trigger responses in Washington that might appear unjustified by more broadly based reporting. One element of an embassy, for example, may report a single conversation hinting at a change in government in an important country. In sensitive Washington, that might be enough to trigger statements or instructions to the ambassador to make inquiries that, under such circumstances, might be unwise. If Washington had waited for other reporting the situation might have seemed less alarmist. Intelligence agencies have a tendency to paint a picture darkly in order to be protected if "the worst happens."

Such reports need often to be balanced by other sources. The presentation of a true evaluation of conditions and prospects for a country by a diplomatic mission depends on the motivation of the source, the circumstances of the revelation, and the "truth" in a larger context. Some information may be given to an embassy officer inadvertently; others may deliberately pass on an item, knowing that it will be reported to Washington. What is their motivation for sharing the information? Are they genuinely worried about the situation? Are they angling for what they believe might be U.S. support for their political ambitions? Are they looking for a favor in return? Are they seeking to discredit other friends of the embassy?

American diplomats in the field are frequently the targets of individuals with a personal agenda. Few of these persons approach diplomats unless they want something themselves, whether it is to assert their point of view or their version of events or to ingratiate themselves with the Americans in anticipation of future requests for help. A few may share information because they believe in what the U.S. represents, sometimes at the risk of their lives. Some try to sweeten the approach with gifts. Diplomats live in realms that are conspiratorial, cynical, and devious. Many sources believe the United States has more power over their lives than may be the case. The U.S. passion for information reinforces this impression.

In pre-Qaddafi Libya, a friend shared with me and with the CIA representative the information that one of the prominent politicians had been a Communist Party member while a student in Italy. Our checking through available sources provided no confirmation. Our friend was also a potential candidate for political office. We had to assume he was discrediting a rival and therefore listened to his allegations with caution. On more than one occasion in each of the countries in which I have served, an ingratiating offer to share important information has been followed by a request to assist a son to get a scholarship to the United States or a friend to acquire a local agency of an American company.

Circumstances are important when judging information. If someone has shared the memorandum of an important conversation involving foreign officials, questions arise: Why is he sharing it? Who wrote the memorandum? Did the writer wish to put one party or another in a favorable light? Is the memorandum authentic? What is the "truth" regarding a country of interest to the United States? Politicians, even in our own country, speak in the context of what they want people to hear, of how they want to appear themselves. Do snippets of negative information add up to general unrest in a country, suggesting radical change? Is one or another of the elements of an embassy unduly pessimistic or unduly sanguine? Have they reached their conclusion to please someone in Washington or because of their confidence in the source? How does one balance predictions of disaster with conditions of apparent calm?

This intense pressure for information inevitably has its effect on how American diplomacy and Americans are seen in many countries abroad. U.S. officials do intrude. If they are doing their job, they are constantly seeking information to meet the actual or presumed Washington requirements. They are doing this sometimes skillfully, sometimes bluntly. It is little wonder that, in sensitive societies not accustomed to this passion for information, diplomats are seen as "spies."

Neither is it surprising that the United States has difficulty abroad in picturing the Soviet diplomats as engaged in espionage when many consider that the United States and most other major powers are involved in the same pursuit. The fact that we see our methods and objectives as different from the Soviets does not change the image.

Americans can only feel—they cannot know—the degree to which the search for data creates resentment among others. In some countries, it is certainly a factor in shaping the attitude of suspicion and hostility toward the United States. In acquiring and reporting information, an American diplomat must tread a path between the obstacles and sensitivities of a foreign environment and the peculiar demands and vulnerabilities of Washington. The path can be difficult and, in times of crisis, dangerous. If the path is not traveled with skill, that fragile link of confidence necessary to an ambassador's success both with the host government and with Washington can be broken. It can result also in a failure in Washington to appreciate the nature and the imminence of a foreign policy crisis.

VII

♪

THE THIRD WORLD

ONE BRIGHT MORNING in October 1940, I sat in a modest room in Wardha in Central India and spoke with Mahatma Gandhi. The slim figure, dressed in dhoti and cotton shawl and reclining on an immaculate white mat, had the magnetism not so much of a god as of an astute politician. He spoke words I have never forgotten: "Someday the British will leave India. Our non-violent movement will lead them to violent acts. They may chop off a million heads, but soon they will tire of chopping heads."

I had spent the previous weekend in Bombay with the Rama Rau family. Lady Rama Rau, a stately Indian woman, was a leader in the Congress Party. Their daughter, Santha, had returned a short time before from school in England. I heard from her the story of her being refused entry at a club in Bombay when taken there by a young British friend, a story she was later to relate in her book *Home to India*.*

The weekend in Bombay and the day in Wardha were my introduction to a movement that was to change much of the face of the world in the following four decades and was to

*Santha Rama Rau, *Home to India* (New York and London: Harper and Brothers, 1944).

dominate my life and those of many an American diplomat: the transition from empires to independent countries. Many Americans—business representatives, journalists, teachers, and missionaries—were familiar with conditions in the colonial territories. Most people in the United States, however, were only vaguely informed of the movements for independence in an imperial world taken for granted on the colored maps in American school rooms. Fewer still knew the personalities who were to emerge as leaders in a new group of countries: Ho Chi Minh, building a network in Paris in the 1920s; or the founders of the Indian Congress Party or the Moslem League, gathering to press their case in London in the 1930s; or Kwame Nkrumah, talking of African independence at Lincoln University in Pennsylvania in the 1940s—all were unknown in the United States.

During the 1950s and 1960s, the creation of new states affected more than half of the population of the world. Suddenly a "Third World" emerged that acted and reacted in unexpected ways. Nations that might otherwise have been considered peripheral to U.S. interests became a major arena for the U.S. confrontation with the Soviets. Turmoil and revolution in weak and distant nations became the substance of bitter debates in the United States; U.S. interests were suddenly involved, largely because the Soviet Union seemed to be involved.

Many in the United States and in the new lands challenge the term Third World. They prefer to speak of emerging nations, developing nations, less developed nations, underdeveloped nations. Certainly the nations that form the Third World vary greatly in size, strength, and character. Not all are newly independent. In the Middle East, the former mandates, such as Iraq, emerged from a quasi-independent status. The Latin American countries that consider themselves part of this Third World have not been colonies since the early nineteenth century.

Nevertheless, a common thread of shared experience—or

imagined experience—unites a South Korea, an Argentina, an India, a Rwanda, and a Saudi Arabia. They share a sense of being disadvantaged in the past by the political or economic domination of an outside—Western—power. The early leaders of the postwar independence movements had known each other in world capitals, sometimes in exile. Together they had built visions of their own independence and of their common goals in a world of new nations. Even in the earliest days of these movements, they resented efforts by outsiders to divide them or differentiate among them.

As Americans became aware of the creation of this Third World, they had many questions about the attitudes of the new nations and the issues that emerged from their creation. Why are these nations not democratic? Why do they seem to oppose us on so many issues? Why don't they see the Soviet threat as we see it?

The answers lie in the contrasting perspectives of the United States and the new nations: Americans had illusions about the nature of the independence struggle based on their own history; leaders in the new nations, reading the same history, had unrealistic expectations of the United States. To compound the separation in attitudes, the United States and the Third World saw the Soviet Union in different lights. Related issues arose not only between Washington and the newly independent nations, but between Washington and America's European allies as well. The task fell to the American diplomats to bridge the gaps in understanding among the United States, the new nations, and the Europeans created by these differing national approaches to the independence movement.

Americans looked at the twentieth century movement toward independence as if it were 1776 all over again. They expected the emergence of countries that would identify with the United States. They looked for the creation of democratic institutions and for respect for the rights of the individual. When the Third World did not develop along this path, Americans were disappointed, irritated, and disillusioned. As a result, ironically, the United States, which had so often reminded the world of its former colonial status, found it more difficult to understand and relate to the new nations than the former imperial powers.

A close examination of the history of the United States and that of the new nations of this century reveals the error of the American perception. The American Revolution of 1776 was far removed in character, as well as time, from what has happened in the past 40 years. In matters of institutions, concepts, race, social conditions, and economies, the experiences differ widely.

Many of the leaders of the new countries did find inspiration in the writings of the American revolution. Their independence movements, like 1776, were against domination by an outside power. Echoes of the same chauvinism, bombast, and sensitivity that characterized the young American republic can be found in many of the new nations. The differences, however, have proven to be more fundamental than the similarities.

Take the matter of the development of indigenous political institutions. By 1776 the United States had had 150 years of development of political and judicial institutions. Although based on the British model, the legislatures of the thirteen colonies were adapted to the special circumstances and feelings of the New World. Democratic institutions, including the recognition of human rights and an independent judiciary, were well implanted by the time of American independence. This has seldom been the case in the new nations of this century.

The roots of European political influence went deep in only a few countries of the Third World. Although India had its own traditions of democracy in the village *panchayets*, 150 years of British influence undoubtedly helped establish national democracy in that country. Africa was a different story. Belgian rule lasted barely two generations and little effort was made to prepare the peoples of the Belgian Congo (later Zaire) for independence. German rule was wiped out without a trace. British rule was short-lived in most of their African colonies. The Portuguese stayed the longest, but did little to develop local political structures. France has maintained a strong position largely by not seeking to implant French-style governments in Africa. In Asia and Africa, where pre-colonial regimes existed, they were likely to be autocratic, whether kingdoms, sultanates, or tribal structures. Colonial powers often maintained these structures and ruled indirectly through them.

Despite the lack of democratic tradition, when independence came the European power, often under the pressure of public opinion at home, sought to create the structure of democracy. Constitutions, prime ministers, parliaments, independent judiciaries, and elections existed in name, but largely as facades for single-party or one man rule. In many cases, in time, the Westminster institutions were dropped and government changed into a form described by those in power as more befitting the political requirements and traditions of the country.

During the colonial period, the laws and regulations by which the colony was administered were often highly authoritarian. The new country might let the institutions of democracy slip into decline, but the colonial administrative laws were retained. The true legacy of the colonial period in most places was not democratic, but authoritarian. The new leaders found the emergency powers, arbitrary arrest, and indefinite incarceration more useful than the thinly established democratic structure. When, in addition, the new rulers turned back to more authentic local traditions, they turned back to traditions that were fundamentally autocratic.

The birth pangs of many of the new nations were often difficult. Internal conflicts that had been hidden or suppressed during the colonial period erupted or became more acute. Severe problems of economic development and finances arose. In such cases, the new government returned, of apparent necessity, to centralized autocratic rule as internal stability, development, and order became high priorities.

Finally, in countries in which personalities have been more important than institutions, the shape of politics emerged to glorify the personality. Leaders came forward out of imprisonment or exile, and assumed power by direct transfer from the metropole. Elections became the means of confirming the authority of the dominant personality and his or her group, not of selecting them. Given the internal rivalries, new leaders became acutely sensitive to threats of opposition and often suppressed rivals and their followers ruthlessly. In the process, leaders took on more and more the trappings of a glorified one-man rule. Americans were shocked by growing corruption and authoritarian methods, even in friendly countries.

To Americans, freedom means respect for the individual and his rights, the freedom to decide on laws and the application of laws by democratic means, and freedom of enterprise and trade. Strong political institutions have been developed in the United States incorporating principles of individual choice and political expression.

Freedom in the new countries is essentially freedom from the rule and presence of a nation of a different race; the concept encompasses independence for a people or a group, rather than an individual. The population in many of the new countries is prepared to submit to authoritarian leadership, provided it is their leadership. A labored and pressured national consensus is to be preferred to a divisive vote.

A fundamental difference exists in the concept of government. The founding fathers in the new United States regarded government as a necessary evil. They had other interests—as farmers, lawyers, merchants. There were then—and have always been in American society—socially acceptable alternatives to the position and power of governmental office. This has not been true in most of the new nations. Except in the most advanced of the newly independent countries, the path to prestige, power, and often wealth lies mainly through governmental, including military, positions. Commerce and business in general have been the prerogative of a minority, and sometimes a despised minority. The newly educated class was educated for ruling. The houses, the cars, the titles, the perquisites of the former colonial civilian and military officials were the coveted symbols of position and power. To lose one's position in government was to risk losing one's favored position in society—and, perhaps, one's life. Far from seeking to leave government, those in the newer nations cling tenaciously to positions of governmental power.

In the early American republic, the army that won the revolution could not wait to demobilize. In many of the new countries, on the contrary, the army remains a fundamental source of power. As civilian rulers quarrel or governmental facades crumble, the army steps in to preserve national unity. In societies that have fundamentally authoritarian traditions, this step is understood and often welcomed and respected.

In America a transplanted people revolted against the rulers of their own ethnic stock. Race was not a factor. Eighty-two percent of the colonial population in 1780 was of white European origin. By contrast, every independence movement since World War II has been by an indigenous race against rulers of another race. Race has been a major element in the formation of the attitudes of the new nations toward the United States and Europe. They have reacted to what they see as an ethnocentric view of the world in the developed Western nations, a view that is basically contemptuous of those of other regions and races.

The American colonists saw themselves as Englishmen and initially as fighting for the rights of Englishmen in North America. Only after they were refused treatment as Englishmen did they strike for independence. In contrast, the populations of the newly independent nations of today never wanted to be Englishmen, Frenchmen, Belgians, Portuguese.

They started out by wanting to recapture their indigenous heritage; with few exceptions, they had little interest in preserving what was alien to them. The independence movements of the twentieth century were not only against political and economic domination, they were also against the humiliation of racial discrimination.

In North America in 1776 there may have been strong feelings against many British and against Tories. There were, however, no clubs that excluded Americans of European origin. There were no areas of cities cordoned off for Europeans only. There were no institutions to engender, in the leaders of the new American nation, the deep feelings of hurt pride and resentment that nineteenth and twentieth century colonial practices bred in many in Asia and Africa.

There were marked differences, too, in education. Although each of the thirteen colonies had different traditions, all had developed educational institutions and relatively high literacy rates. Flourishing universities were already established on an American model. Americans from New Hampshire to Georgia spoke one language. At independence, many of the new nations had inadequately developed educational systems and high rates of illiteracy. Universities, if they existed, were often modeled along European lines, with curricula that had little relationship to local needs and circumstances. A country as large as Zaire had eight high school graduates and no university graduates at the time of independence. All of the major new countries except Indonesia had—and still have—major problems in deciding on a national language.

Economically, in 1776, the population of slightly under four million, including half a million slaves and perhaps 300,000 Indians, was on the edge of a vast undeveloped continent. Population density was 4.5 persons to the square mile. Per capita income was relatively high for the standards of the day. Though mercantilism still prevailed, the United States was manufacturing a substantial part of its own requirements, helped by a cadre of skilled manpower. Technical innovations of worldwide significance were being launched in an atmosphere of optimistic experimentation. The new nations of today are, by contrast, frequently plagued with overpopulation, unemployment, and underemployment and with a lack of the skills necessary for development. Further, at a time when independence brought new needs for infrastructure and support, revenues sometimes declined and subsidies ended. The new leaders faced the frustration of enormous economic problems and pressures, at times aggravated by famine, drought, and malnutrition, unlike anything that faced the young American republic. Some, as students, had been attracted to Marxism and were tempted to try radical, socialist solutions.

Despite these basic differences, many of the leaders in the new nations still saw parallels with the United States. Politicians in the new nations were familiar not only with the writings of Jefferson and with the details of Wilson's pledges on self-determination, but also with the routine declarations that American leaders have issued pledging support for freedom throughout the world. As they faced the new economic problems, they saw a parallel with the Marshall Plan and with the generous U.S. contributions to the reconstruction of Europe. Third World nations looked at U.S. policies against this background and developed unrealistic hopes both for U.S. economic assistance and political support for the remaining anticolonial causes.

In the economic field, given these expectations, the response of the United States to the needs of the developing world was disappointing. As a subsequent chapter will point out, the disappointment was due both to the levels and the complexities of aid. Under intense pressure from populations that had expected miracles at the time of independence, the new nations in the late 1960s sought to mobilize, primarily under Algerian leadership, to press for a "new international economic order." Hampered by the realities of their internal situations, they turned to concentrate on what they considered the external inequities in the distribution of the world's wealth. The United States was considered central to a solution to the world economic problems and the heat of the frustration of the new nations was directed at Washington. While other nations, including the Europeans, equivocated in their response to Third World demands, the United States took firm positions against what it considered unrealistic positions on resource transfer, debt, commodity prices, technology transfer, and the reorganization of the world's primary financial institutions.

To many U.S. diplomats working in the developing countries, these were basically political issues wrapped in economic terms. They felt that the United States did not need to be so negative in its responses because no clear consensus existed among the Third World nations on how to resolve these issues. The frontal opposition of the United States, primarily centered in the Treasury Department, gave the developing nations the opportunity to join in attacking the American position and to avoid facing up to their own differences on such issues as technology transfer and debt.

In 1976, Henry Kissinger, then secretary of state, spoke on the New International Economic Order in Kansas City. Although his speech recognized the validity of many of the Third World grievances, he twice remarked: "The old economic order has served us very well." It was my task in Jakarta at the time to present the speech to the Indonesians as a positive step forward in the U.S. approach on this issue. When I did so, I received the response, "Yes, that shows movement on the part of the United States. But why did Dr. Kissinger have to say, not once but twice, that the old economic order had served well? That is the heart of the issue; we do not agree." When I returned to the United States on consultation, I asked the assistant secretary of state for economic affairs, who had helped draft the speech, why that phrase had been inserted. "That," he replied, "was the price of getting Treasury to clear the speech."

The confrontation with the United States was also inspired, in part, by the growth of the Organization of Producing and Exporting Countries (OPEC) and the influence of this cartel on oil prices. Even countries harmed by its policies refrained from criticizing OPEC because they saw, as one Asian minister said to me, "OPEC is the locomotive leading the rest of us to economic improvement."

The disappointment of the Third World countries at the U.S. response to their economic needs was matched by a disappointment over the U.S. response on political issues. Leaders of independence movements had expected to find the United States their greatest champion in opposition to European colonialism. They felt that Americans would understand, more than others, their emphasis on national sovereignty and national dignity. They found, instead, an America that seemed more supportive of the colonial powers and of the status quo.

The leaders of the new nations were frequently charismatic personalities and spellbinding orators who helped create an environment of confrontation. Once independent, they pictured their problems as lying in the previous policies of colonialism and their salvation as coming through revolution against colonial institutions. Although the United States was not an imperial power, the focus of attack was against America because of earlier expectations, the perceived American influence over Europe, and the global strength of the United States.

Americans were not prepared for the advent and style of leaders like Sukarno, Nkrumah, Toure, and Nasser. Even after independence, they followed styles developed during the struggle against the colonial power, styles reflecting their sensitivities, their pride, their commitment to changing an old order. Many Americans saw them as mad, impractical, and dangerous. Neither were Americans prepared for the paranoia about discrimination and the growing tendency to blame the United States for all ills.

The views of the more extreme of the Third World nations began with the premise that the United States was seeking to impose its will on the former colonies through an exercise of its military and economic power. The CIA was seen as omnipresent. U.S. altruism and efforts to resolve problems were not viewed as expressions of good faith but as ways to implement U.S. designs. This interpretation of U.S. policy designs resulted, in some countries, in inflexible opposition to U.S. positions and, in others, in an attitude that more could be extracted from the United States by strident demands. Few of the extremist nations in the Third World understood the U.S. system.

As they dealt with these issues, many of the new nations expressed rhetorical and political sympathy with violence and revolution. Movements seeking "liberation" from colonial powers automatically gained broad sympathy. The strong support in the Third World for movements that were seen in the United States as "terrorist" further widened the gap in perspective on world issues. The American attitude, prior to the changes in Portuguese policy, precluded any recognition, for example, of the independence movements in the Portuguese territories in Africa. The new nations saw the Palestinian movement as analogous to their own independence struggle and, in contrast to the U.S. attitude, gave strong support to the Palestine Liberation Organization.

The sharp differences in perspective between the United States and the new nations became most apparent in the United Nations. When the United Nations was formed, the United States dominated its proceedings. Until the early 1960s, Washington could work its will in the General Assembly as well as in the Security Council. As the move toward independence progressed, the UN General Assembly, in which there was no major power veto, came to be dominated more and more by Third World countries and issues. The United States, instead of staying in control, found itself more and more isolated. U.S. diplomacy at the UN became one of "limiting damage" rather than advancing interests.

Critics in the United States saw the United Nations as less and less attentive to U.S. interests. By detailing the vote counts in the General Assembly they sought to show that most of the UN members were on the "wrong side." Congress reduced budget allocations. The debate over the future U.S. relationship to the UN was dominated by demands for withdrawal and for a more strident U.S. counterattack to criticism in the General Assembly, pointing up the hypocrisies, inconsistencies, and weaknesses in the developing world.

The problems for the United States, however, were less related to the United Nations than they were to two issues that for many years have dominated UN proceedings: Southern Africa and the Arab-Israeli dispute. In both, the United States has been largely isolated, not only from the Third World nations but from its European allies as well. To the new nations of the world, these were anticolonial issues. The positions that the United States took on these issues in New York were determined in part by strong domestic pressures and by the assumption in Washington that the United States could exert a constructive influence to curb conflict and resolve problems. Representatives of the United States in the United Nations continually responded to rhetorical attacks by attempting to point out the realistic limits of U.S. power and proposing what seemed to the Americans to be feasible paths to solutions. This approach did not satisfy the demands of America's opponents.

The United States not only felt a responsibility toward the solutions of these regional issues, but saw them also in the context of the global confrontation with the Soviet Union. The Soviet Union, in the U.S. view, had little direct responsibility in the ultimate solution of any of these problems. Moscow could, therefore, stand on the sidelines and exploit the differences with the United States. Some in the United States talked of the Soviets "winning" the struggle for the Third World. The advantages gained by the Soviets and the Cubans in Angola and Mozambique were regarded by many Americans as part of a plan of global aggression. In Libya and Ethiopia (as in Nicaragua), the overthrow of unpopular regimes was seen as Soviet gains. U.S. policymakers, through several administrations, called for corrections in Soviet "behavior" and Soviet "restraint" in the Third World. The Soviets responded that the issues were only between the Soviet Union and these countries. The Soviets had their own list of countries in which they could, on a reciprocal basis, call for U.S. restraint.

The new nations, often weak and insecure in their untried sovereignty, did not want the complications of involvement in the struggle between the superpowers. To them, Soviet activities in support of "liberation movements" represented appropriate support for an anticolonial cause. The only allies of interest were those who would pledge unequivocal allegiance to this anticolonial struggle. Communist parties with their supportive rhetoric and organizational capacity were frequently among such allies. Zhou Enlai was seen as a special hero at the initial gathering of the "non-aligned" at Bandung, in Indonesia, in 1955. The concept of "non-alignment" had a strong appeal; after the break between Yugoslavia and the Soviet Union, non-alignment found a powerful champion in Marshal Tito.

The rise of the Non-Aligned Movement created one additional issue between the United States and the Third World. Non-alignment appeared to equate the international ambitions and conduct of the United States with those of the Soviet Union. The United States was not prepared for this "plague on both your houses" attitude. Its resentment toward this approach deepened as the new nations, in the United Nations and in other multinational fora, seemed to grow more bitter against the United States than against the Soviet

Union. Non-alignment seemed to become non-alignment only against the United States. John Foster Dulles called it "immoral."

The differing perspectives growing out of the end of empires thus created issues between the United States and the Third World. The process of decolonization also created problems with America's European allies. The United States and Europe came out of World War II with differing attitudes toward the European colonial empires. While Britain realistically contemplated the need to grant independence, at least in India, the French, the Belgians, the Dutch, and the Portuguese did not have similar outlooks toward their colonial territories. The United States, while ideologically committed to decolonization, was concerned about potential instability and other conditions that might favor communist activity. In other situations, considered more secure, the United States often wished to move more rapidly toward independence than the former colonial powers. Except where Soviet influence appeared to be a threat, the United States felt that a peaceful grant of independence was preferable to a bitter conflict between a European power and an independence movement that would only provide opportunities for communist exploitation.

Europeans played upon American fears of communism to seek U.S. support for the retention of their empires. The French encouraged Americans to regard the war in Vietnam as part of the anti-Soviet struggle, rather than part of a decolonization process. The Portuguese stressed the importance to NATO of bases in the Azores to discourage American support for Angolan and Mozambiquan independence; the aftermath still plagues the United States.

Where independence was granted, Americans often found to their surprise that the former colonial power was regarded more favorably than the United States. Britain and France in particular, despite their colonial history, were closer to many of the new countries and better understood their attitudes and the interests involved. The Europeans, especially the French, knew how to maintain ties and influence with their former colonies. The French, learning the lessons of history, compensated for their serious mistakes in South East Asia and Algeria by a highly sophisticated attitude toward the new Francophone African nations. Their new relationship was based on a calculated determination of French interests, a recognition of African sensitivities and pride, particularly in the matter of race, a recognition of the individual differences among states, a willingness to adapt to political change, a consistency of economic support, and personal attention to the individual rulers. U.S. diplomats in Africa had great difficulty in arranging even a few minutes for an African leader with a president of the United States. In contrast, the French rolled out a red carpet, arranged ostentatious ceremonial events, and, always, an official lunch or dinner and meeting with the French president.

In this series of confrontations on Third World issues, it fell to U.S. diplomats to work not only in new, strange, and sometimes dangerous environments, but also to explain policies that were often bitterly assailed by those in the new nations caught up in their internal frustrations and in regional disputes. In contrast to parts of the world where the United States was seen as an ally, U.S. diplomats in Third World countries faced charges of cultural and economic imperialism, egregious intervention, and racism. For many officials in Washington, the experience was searing; the charges and the political environments out of which they grew were considered illogical and incomprehensible. The Third World became an area to be scorned, distrusted, attacked. The diplomats had to accomplish the task of explaining and assessing trends without seeming parochial to unsympathetic listeners at home and while keeping open credible access in the countries in which they lived.

The diplomat was thus in the middle between two very different perspectives. American policymakers and diplomats were trained in languages and in attitudes to work in a Euro-centricworld. American diplomacy in the Third World required a new kind of style—less formal, more personal. If, despite policy differences, the United States was to enjoy a position of respect in new countries, it would come about through the personal attention and sensitivity of individual Americans, including diplomats.

In part, the difficulty that Americans have in gaining a true assessment of the feelings of peoples in the Third World arises from a problem of communication. Many in the newly independent nations are culturally conditioned to tell the American visitors what they want to hear—about the Soviets, about free enterprise, about Israel, and about U.S. policies. Not only does this calculated approach by those in the developing world serve the polite needs of hospitality, but it is also a way of gaining American support. Leaders otherwise isolated in Africa, such as Tshombe in Katanga, Ojukwo in Biafra, and Savimbi in Angola, have, with the help of U.S. public relations firms, said the things Americans like to hear. The danger of hearing only what one wants to hear is that one will never know what the people of another culture are truly thinking and feeling.

An Africanist wrote these words: "Please let me stress, never make the mistake of thinking the African is a simple soul, open and frank. . . . most Africans, have for generations let the Europeans penetrate so far and no further into their thoughts and culture. If you encounter a truly simple, frank soul, he is likely to be an idiot. The other open, laughing, gay people you meet are concealing one hell of a lot and it's going to take you a long time to get to know them well enough to find out what it is."

Many Americans fail to understand the Third World because they do not listen to the voices of those countries. Ali Mazrui, a Kenyan writer, in an essay entitled, "Uncle Sam's Hearing Aid," writes: "Americans are brilliant communicators, but bad listeners. Because Americans can communicate effectively, the rest of humanity is, to some extent, becoming Americanized. But because Americans are bad listeners, they have resisted being humanized, in the sense of learning to respond to the needs and desires of the rest of the world."*

This chapter has concentrated on the issues that have—often to the bewilderment of some Americans—separated the United States from the new nations of the twentieth century. The problems have been many, but, as the century closes, the basic issues that followed the thrust for independence may be fading. There is no doubt that the nations of the Third World have turned from their earlier preoccupation with global issues and their readiness to react instantly, strongly, and adversely to U.S. policies. Many of the decolonization issues that sparked earlier manifestations have been resolved. The group solidarity that once existed has been shattered by quarrels and divisions. The Soviet alternative is now seen by many as either menacing or unprofitable. In every continent, profound problems of economic survival and political cohesion have caused nations to turn inward.

Still the gap that U.S. diplomacy must bridge remains, manifested in the issues of human rights, reaction to change, the new phenomenon of terrorism, and assistance in economic development.

*In Sanford J. Ungar, ed., *Estrangement: America and the World* (New York: Oxford University Press, 1985.

VIII

✒

THE DIPLOMACY OF
HUMAN RIGHTS

No PART OF THE foreign affairs agenda involves Americans more deeply in the affairs of the Third World countries than their concern over human rights. When U.S. intervention has been successful, it has saved lives, moderated brutality, and maintained the credibility of America's democratic ideals. When intervention has failed, it has created unrealizable expectations among the oppressed, bitterness at the apparent inconsistency of policy, and resentment at the intrusion of the United States.

Depending on one's point of view, President Jimmy Carter is either blamed or praised for the emphasis on human rights in U.S. diplomacy. An active U.S. diplomatic interest in how other governments treat their people, however, did not begin with Carter. The tradition goes back to the earliest days of a republic founded and nurtured by those seeking freedom from oppression elsewhere. The impulse is deep in the American society.

The Holocaust, the brutality of Stalin, and the suppression of free societies in Eastern Europe following World War II created a renewed consciousness of the depredations of oppressive regimes. The presence of countless refugees fanned the flames of conscience. The U.S. civil rights movement added a domestic element. Many workers involved in obtaining greater rights for the black population in the United States expanded their interest and activities to seek improvement in oppressive conditions elsewhere. They demanded the support of the U.S. government and its diplomatic representatives in this effort. They participated, as members of Congress, congressional staff, and the executive, in the promotion of international human rights policies.

Many Americans who had lived abroad were increasingly conscious that the history and political rhetoric of the United States had raised expectations that their country would help the victims of oppression. As noted in the last chapter, people in the newly independent nations were surprisingly familiar with the words of Jefferson, Lincoln, Wilson, and Roosevelt. Each time a U.S. president spoke of the nation's dedication to the cause of freedom, he heightened this expectation. The words were echoed daily by the Voice of America and the U.S. media.

More and more, programs of military sales and concessional assistance in countries with poor human rights records seemed inconsistent with the ideals Americans were proclaiming. Programs seen as "support" for such regimes conveyed the impression that the United States condoned repressive internal actions. U.S. policies appeared at times to be undercutting more just and democratic aspirations in the developing and Latin American worlds.

This issue was more than humanistic or moral. It was strategic and political as well. As regimes fell with which the United States had been identified, Americans found themselves expelled and excluded by those who followed in China, Iraq, Libya, Nicaragua, and Iran. It was soon clear that oppression created weakness, not strength, and that U.S. identification with oppression created opportunities for adversaries. If U.S. interests were to be adequately protected in strategic areas of the world, the United States needed to give attention not only to the military and economic factors, but to the social and judicial aspects as well.

These demands for more active policies came in the early 1970s at a time when congressional committees were assuming greater power and were attentive to the political power of student protests and rights marches. The Vietnam experience added to this pressure.

At the same time, the collapse of fledgling democratic regimes and internecine violence in the newly independent nations added to American concerns and demands for action. The mantle of colonialism had shielded the United States from some of the deep tensions of societies in Africa and Asia, in places such as Burundi, the Sudan, and southern Africa. Americans wanted their government to do something to improve conditions in these countries.

In the early 1970s, Congress emerged as a significant influence in the promotion of diplomatic efforts on behalf of human rights. Congressman Donald Fraser of Minnesota became chairman of a subcommittee of the House Foreign Affairs Committee responsible for international organizations. Given the broad involvement of international organizations in the promotion of human rights and the responsibility of the House Committee over the authorization of foreign assistance, Fraser used the subcommittee post to create a substantial body of law that mandated U.S. diplomatic involvement in human rights problems in other countries. Not only was all police assistance to foreign countries banned, but military assistance was made contingent upon a satisfactory human rights record. Economic assistance, export credits, and the U.S. position on loans by international financial institutions were to be affected by the human rights circumstances in recipient countries. The Department of State was required to file annual, public reports on human

rights conditions. At first this requirement was only for countries that were aid recipients but it was later extended to all
countries that were members of the United Nations.

Fraser and his staff succeeded in getting this substantial
body of human rights legislation enacted at a time when the
mood of the country favored an activist diplomacy in this
field. He was helped by a broad feeling in the Congress that
the Nixon administration was indifferent to human rights
concerns. The many supporters in Congress of civil rights
legislation were enthusiastic about applying the same principles in U.S. relations with other countries. Other members,
given the sentiment in the country, did not want to appear to
say "no" to a worthy policy. The legislation codified a national
empathy with oppressed peoples and gave impetus to an
active U.S. diplomacy directed at correcting abuses in other
countries. How this legislative pressure worked out in practice is discussed later in this chapter.

Support for an active diplomacy on behalf of human
rights was by no means unanimous within the United States.
Few initiatives in American diplomacy have been as controversial. Although general agreement exists in principle that
the United States should express its concern over abuses
abroad, there is far less agreement over the exact situations in
which Washington should bring its influence to bear.

A national consensus supports policies that seek the freedom of dissidents in the Soviet Union and Eastern Europe,
support for the emigration of Jewish communities, and pressure for a lessening of the Soviet influence on governments
and societies in Eastern Europe. Added to this has been the
desire in the United States to afford a refuge not only to those
who have been the victims of Soviet domination, but also to
those religious and ethnic communities in Europe and
around the world that may still be in danger of further per-
secution.

If Americans disagree over the pursuit of human rights
diplomacy in the Soviet Union and Eastern Europe, the dis-

agreements are either about the effectiveness of our diplomacy or about the relationship of our actions to other objectives of U.S. policies toward the Soviet Union. President Carter was sharply criticized because he would not receive Alexander Solzhenitzyn at the White House at a time when Carter was seeking better relations with the Soviet Union. The debate over the Jackson-Vanick amendment, enacted in 1974 to link most favored nation trade status to Jewish emigration, was more over the means than the ends.

Americans can identify relatively easily with a dissident in the Soviet Union. No sympathy exists for the Soviet regime. The oppression is indisputable. Empathy with the bearded and barefoot revolutionary, shouting under banners in a Third World country, is harder to evoke.

Primary opposition to diplomatic efforts on behalf of human rights in non-communist countries came from those in both the Congress and the private sector who believed that such efforts threatened other interests, particularly security and trade. Representatives of friendly regimes with doubtful human rights records worked hard in the United States to create and build these doubts. Personable, English-speaking personalities, often from wealthy families and with strong friends in the United States, including the Congress, found many Americans willing to accept their rationalization that human rights violations are necessary in the fight against terrorism and communism.

Controversy has thus swirled around the official U.S. attitude toward "friendly" nations that also oppose communism, but whose governments are guilty of human rights violations. Americans primarily concerned with human rights in the Soviet Union have believed that oppression in non-communist countries has been exaggerated, while violations of human rights in the Soviet Union have escaped serious criticism. Such critics believe that weakening non-communist regimes by pressures and criticisms could adversely affect the strategic balance. Jeane Kirkpatrick's controversial article in *Commentary** drew a distinction between *totalitarian* (communist) and *authoritarian* (non-communist) that became, for a time, an important doctrine in the debate over diplomatic support for human rights.

Such arguments have led to charges of inconsistency in the implementation of human rights policies. The United States is allegedly harsh on those weak friendly countries over which it has a measure of influence, but spares the Soviet Union or strong friendly nations in which substantial security interests are involved. Critics have laid the collapse of such regimes as those in Iran and Nicaragua to U.S. pressure to reform human rights practices.

U.S. diplomacy in favor of human rights suffers inevitably from the contradictions between promise and fulfillment. The frequent references in U.S. domestic political rhetoric to human dignity, democracy, and freedom raise expectations that America will indeed work to create these conditions in other lands. In an extreme case, I have had Kurdish tribesmen in the north of Iraq quote to me President Wilson's Fourteen Points in favor of self-determination and then ask why we have not arranged to create an independent Kurdish nation.

With the expectation that the United States will fulfill its rhetorical promises goes often a belief abroad that America has the capacity to change other societies or to change governments; only a lack of resolve to do so stands in the way. U.S. diplomats are constantly placed in the position of seeking to explain the realistic limits of U.S. influence in another society to those who believe we are truly omnipotent.

Business interests have opposed the use of economic sanctions and the linkage of export credits to human rights as being harmful to U.S. business while failing to improve a local situation. This argument has been particularly strong in the case of South Africa, where proponents of U.S. business have pointed to the positive role of such business in enhanc-

*Commentary 68 (November 1979):34-45.

ing the opportunities for the black population of that country. Subsequent events in South Africa, however, have resulted in the enactment of sanctions against South Africa by the U.S. Congress in 1986 and a growing withdrawal of companies.

The strong national support for the inclusion of human rights in our diplomatic agenda was demonstrated at the advent of the Reagan administration. Although Republican campaign rhetoric spoke of moving away from the emphasis of the Carter presidency, the new administration found that both the laws and public attitudes compelled it to continue an active interest in human rights around the world. That active interest in turn will continue to involve U.S. diplomats in the most sensitive aspects of other societies and governments. While the interest is continuous, the changes in mood and administrations within the United States affect the implementation of that diplomacy abroad.

When administrations change, those nations resisting official U.S. pressure to reform internal policies look for evidence that the new American leadership will support a more tolerant view of their internal actions. Such signals give them hope that they will not have to make the difficult if not dangerous internal political moves that may be necessary to satisfy the United States. In South Africa, for example, decisions were postponed in the latter days of the Carter administration in the hope that the Reagan administration would be less concerned with questions of apartheid. Over time, this judgment on the part of some in South Africa proved to be incorrect.

Presidents themselves can cause confusion. During official visits, presidents like to accentuate the positive, at times to the detriment of other objectives. President Carter praised the shah of Iran as "an island of stability" at a time when the U.S. ambassador was seeking to bring home to the government of Iran the dangers inherent in their treatment of individuals.* Vice President George Bush appeared to praise

*New York Times, Jan. 1, 1980.

Philippine democracy in Manila during a visit to President Marcos at a time when the Reagan administration was urging reform.* It is not surprising that foreigners at times are confused about the purposes of our diplomacy. An ambassador can take some steps on personal initiative; such steps are not likely to be credible if senior officials of the government are saying something else. Against a background of sometimes conflicting official statements, newspaper articles, and unofficial visitors reflecting widely divergent views on human rights policy, the U.S. diplomat must seek to influence a foreign government to change policies that it may consider essential to its power and security.

In human rights diplomacy, the conflict is not only over policies; it is also over facts. Advocacy organizations may claim violations that cannot be independently confirmed, or may exaggerate those that can be confirmed. Any diplomat approaching a government on a sensitive issue must be certain of the facts that prompt the approach. In circumstances in which emotions are high, political futures are at stake, and exaggerations are common, seeking out the facts can be extremely difficult, if not impossible. The search for information in itself is sensitive. Sources must be protected, and yet credibility must be established—especially if a diplomat is to discuss a precise situation with local authorities.

Efforts to correct human rights violations in authoritarian countries often represent a direct challenge to activities that keep a leader in office. In nations where violations occur, the traditions are often byzantine and brutal. The stakes are high. I have had rulers explain candidly to me, when I have raised questions of torture, that to stop such practices would require actions against security services on which their own lives and power depend. The involvement of outsiders in discouraging such practices strikes directly at the most basic concern of a political leader: survival. The survival involved is not only

*New York Times, July 1, 1981.

that of the ruler. Authoritarian rulers gather around them family members, business associates, and military cronies who not only help sustain power, but benefit from that power as well. Any threat to the ruler is a threat to them. They encourage resistance to outside pressures for reform.

When I was ambassador to the Philippines in 1977, I was instructed on several occasions to raise with President Marcos the possibility of releasing Benigno Aquino from imprisonment. (Aquino, a political rival of Marcos, was then being held under a death sentence. He was subsequently released to go to the United States for medical treatment, but upon his return to Manila was assassinated.) In the days when I raised the question of Aquino with Marcos, he always discussed the issue with me in measured terms. Mrs. Marcos and others around the president, however, made very clear their anger at my involvement in this affair.

The effectiveness of U.S. diplomacy in the field of human rights has been aided by the fact that most nations are sensitive to how the outside world looks at their internal practices. Idi Amin and Jean Bedel Bokassa were exceptions. Depending on the way the subject is approached, most nations respond to charges of mistreatment of their citizens, even if they resent the outside intrusion, either with genuine efforts to correct abuses, cosmetic actions to divert attention, or by defending what they are doing.

From the human rights standpoint, alternative regimes may not necessarily be an improvement. The opposition may have the same attitude toward power—and its protection—as the incumbents. They may profess their love for democracy because they are out and the others are in, but that does not change their basic way of looking at the acquisition and maintenance of power. The opposition alternative in repressive regimes may be as tough and unscrupulous as the one in power. Their intention may be to portray themselves in a way that will enlist the support of the United States government in their own cause. A U.S. diplomat seeking to influence a human rights situation must avoid either romanticizing the opposition or becoming involved with any single group. Such diplomats at times face the need to remind a government in Washington attracted to an opposition group that the alternative could prove as unacceptable as the incumbent.

Those foreign officials whom one approaches on human rights issues can at times be remarkably candid about their circumstances. In 1977, the Humphrey-Kennedy amendment was passed by Congress requiring the cessation of all military sales credit to Argentina if that country did not demonstrate visible progress in human rights. Argentina was given until October 1978 to show such progress. As under secretary of state, I was sent to Buenos Aires to determine whether any such progress was possible. At issue were questions of the release of political prisoners and the assumption of responsibility for an undetermined number of persons who had disappeared, apparently at the hands of the security forces. During my discussions in Buenos Aires, I met with General Alveno Eduardo Hargyundeguy, the Minister of Interior. When I raised the question of the disappeared, he waved to a set of filing cabinets along one wall of his office. "We know who the disappeared are," he said. "I have the files right there. But, if we acknowledge this, we will be deluged with legal claims and we cannot countenance that."

The Humphrey-Kennedy amendment was invoked, but after the Falklands war the military junta in Argentina was replaced by a democratic regime. Many of those who supported the new government gave credit to the pressures from the United States as a factor in the change.

Even if diplomatic pressure is not immediately effective, international attention helps focus attention on abuses. Governments, however, will not readily submit to changes that may be seen as submission to the pressures of an outside country.

This raises the question of "quiet diplomacy." Depending on the objective of the diplomatic efforts the diplomat may wish to speak out on the human rights situation in the host country or encourage Washington to do so. In deciding on this approach, the diplomat must weigh whether a statement will diminish the diplomat's own effectiveness on the scene, move a government to take action, or increase its sensitivity to outside pressures and make other diplomatic efforts more difficult. Generally, public statements are used in the diplomacy of human rights when it appears that public pressure may succeed after quiet efforts have not, or when Washington decides that a government is unlikely to carry out reforms. In such a case, the only course for the United States is, by strong public criticism, to "distance" itself by making clear that it supports neither the regime nor its actions. The impact of such statements is, of course, enhanced if they are made at the presidential or cabinet level or if the diplomat can speak for such a level. Official statements can be given further strength by special efforts to make them known through the Voice of America and the other media of the USIA.

One of the most controversial forms of U.S. public pressure on other regimes is the series of human rights reports on individual member nations of the United Nations mandated in legislation in the 1970s. Based on information from embassies and international human rights organizations, these reports are submitted to the Congress and published. The debate each year within the U.S. government over how strongly to criticize a friendly government is intense. Many governments have expressed bitter resentment at this intrusion of the United States into their domestic affairs. Brazil, for example, terminated military cooperation with the United States in 1977 because of displeasure with the U.S. human rights report.

Diplomats can also give public signals of opposition to a regime through conspicuous meetings with opposition leaders or local human rights organizations. Contacts with opposition figures may be strongly opposed by the government, and diplomats may need to resort to indirect approaches.

Such approaches, however accomplished, signal to the people of a country the wider interest of the United States in human rights problems. Efforts to reduce identification with a harsh regime are, of course, more difficult where the United States has major strategic interests and substantial assistance programs.

Whatever the circumstances, a diplomat cannot effectively influence the actions or decisions of another country without access to that country's leaders, decision makers, and opinion molders. The diplomat of the United States often has the advantage that, even if the host country is not sympathetic with the human rights objectives, relations with the United States are important for other reasons such as aid, military security, or traditional ties. Diplomats, however, must weigh carefully the pressure for and frequency of access. In most cases, opportunities for meetings with top officials are limited and other subjects need to be raised as well.

For the American diplomat, the existence of the human rights legislation that came into effect in the 1970s provides both a problem and an opportunity. Many foreign governments with human rights problems consider that the application of U.S. legislative sanctions constitute an unacceptable intrusion into their internal affairs and resist measures that would be seen by their own people as submitting to foreign pressures.

U.S. laws can often be more effective in abeyance than in application. Cases are hard to find in which the actual application of U.S. law has led to changes in the human rights practices of another country. Diplomats can, however, explain the existence—or possibility—of legislation as an indication of the general feeling of the American people on an issue. If this is presented without pressure, diplomatic efforts can be supported.

The legislation enacted in the 1970s gave U.S. administrations the authority and, in some cases, a mandate to apply human rights criteria to programs of military assistance, military sales, police assistance, export credits, trade, and economic assistance programs that did not fall in the category of "basic human needs." These provisions were obvious tools of pressure on foreign governments. The legislation, in many instances, left the interpretation of given situations to the discretion of the administration. This inevitably led to some inconsistency in the application of these laws.

Ideally, a government should be able both to penalize and to reward in support of diplomatic efforts to improve human rights. For the United States, penalties are easier than rewards. Action to terminate an assistance program, to refuse a loan, or to deny military sales is administratively simple even though the decision to do so may be controversial. To reward by reshaping or supplementing assistance programs has been more difficult. The inflexibility of the appropriations process and the cumbersomeness of the administration of U.S. aid programs generally have tended to defeat efforts to "fine tune" assistance in response to corrections in human rights abuses.

In carrying out the human rights mission, the U.S. diplomat frequently has important allies. Many Western European democracies share the concern of the United States over human rights violations both in Eastern Europe and in the Third World. Europeans are particularly attentive to violations in their former colonies. They are less inclined to use economic and military programs for pressure, but they are often prepared to support the United States with diplomatic efforts.

At times, when a foreign government is resistant to bilateral pressures on human rights, that government may be prepared to turn to an international organization. The United Nations, in the General Assembly, the Security Council, and specialized agencies dealing with human rights, has established a strong body of precedents in support of efforts to improve human rights. Of particular importance have been the UN Commission on Human Rights, the organization that has grown out of the Helsinki accords, and regional organizations such as the Inter-American Commission on Human Rights. Turning to an international organization such as the Inter-American Commission on Human Rights can provide a more politically acceptable way for a government to acknowledge and deal with an internal problem.

Private organizations, some of them international in scope, are another source of impartial observations of human rights problems. They are particularly useful where there is disagreement over facts or conditions and an impartial referee is desired. Reports by such organizations as the International Commission of Jurists and the International League of Red Cross Societies have played important roles in bringing human rights violations to the attention of a country's leaders and providing a basis on which to make improvements. Other organizations, such as Amnesty International, do not deal with governments, but create pressures through arousing the concern of private citizens in the United States and abroad. Organizations such as the Lawyers' Committee for Peace Through Law have acted as channels for funds to support the defense of victims of human rights violations.

In the last analysis, the United States can, through its policies, legislation, and diplomatic activity, create pressures, but little is likely to change unless the foreign government decides that change is in its interest. In cases where a government is inclined to correct an abuse, the United States may help in finding a formula for change. Such a case happened while I was ambassador in Indonesia.

Indonesia, in 1965, was the scene of a major political upheaval. Although some still dispute the exact nature of the event, it is generally accepted that communist elements sought to smooth the path for their succession to power by eliminating the top leadership of the Army. The effort backfired and Communist Party members and their sympathizers were rounded up and detained. When I went to Indonesia as ambassador in 1974, some 35,000 suspected members of the

Communist Party or communist-front organizations were still incarcerated. In the United States, this was considered a gross violation of human rights and strong pressures were being exerted to take punitive actions against Indonesia. It was clearly an important item on my diplomatic agenda.

My preliminary soundings on this issue suggested to me that the Indonesians wanted to find a solution, although they were concerned over the possible reception the detainees might receive in their former villages and over their chances for employment. The first step was to get reliable information on the numbers involved and on the conditions of their treatment. To do this, the Indonesians agreed to turn to the International Committee of the Red Cross. The Committee sent observers and filed a report with the Indonesian government. Foreign embassies had access to the information on a privileged basis. In the second step, I worked with other Western diplomatic colleagues in a longer term effort to encourage the Indonesians to prepare a program of release. At the same time, I brought to the attention of an army general, a close associate of President Suharto, the fact that legislation was being considered in the U.S. Congress that might require terminating assistance to Indonesia because of human rights violations. I emphasized that I was informing him of a fact, not in any way threatening the Indonesian government.

Within a few days the general returned. He said that he had discussed the question with other Indonesian officials. They felt that if he were to take my message to Suharto, the president would see it as a threat. Instead they proposed to send a delegation to Washington to talk with those in the Congress concerned with the issue. The delegation, on return, could then report to President Suharto that Indonesia indeed had a problem in the United States and in this way, perhaps, something could be done about the issue.

That was how it turned out. A remarkably astute delegation went to Washington and reached the predicted conclusion. Within a few months a plan had been drawn up for the phased release of the detainees; by 1978 all but a few had been freed. This change was only possible because Indonesia saw the need. The U.S. legislation, perhaps, spurred their consideration of the matter, but that was secondary to their own decision.

As this is being written, the world is observing other improvements in relations between the governed and the governors in many countries and challenges to traditional oppression in others. Efforts from the outside, including those of diplomats of the United States and other democracies, have clearly played a role in heightening the internal awareness of the issues and in establishing the pressures that led to change. The diplomacy of human rights is complex, controversial, sensitive, and not always rewarding. The patterns of change being observed, however, suggest that such diplomacy may be more effective than was realized at the time that the various pressures for such diplomacy were being applied.

IX

℘

THE UNITED STATES AND
POLITICAL CHANGE

THE EARLY MORNING stillness is suddenly broken by the sound of steel shutters being lowered. The few shops that have opened close again. The rumble of tanks can be heard and, perhaps, some shots. People stay in their homes and turn on radios. Martial music and cryptic messages announce a coup in a Third World country. For the U.S. diplomat, the questions from Washington begin immediately: What has happened? Did the embassy know it was going to happen? If not, why not? Who are the new leaders? What is their attitude toward the United States?

In the past 10 years, sudden changes of government have taken place in more than 25 countries. Such change is clearly neither new nor rare, but modern communications have made Americans more conscious than ever of these events. Television brings the drama, the violence, the tragedy, and the new personalities vividly into the nation's living rooms. I have in my career been close to five such unpredicted overthrows. In each one, appreciable U.S. interests were involved, and U.S. diplomacy was faulted for being unable to detect or prevent such occurrences.

111

In 1958, I was the desk officer for Iraq when a military coup overthrew the government of King Faisal. The event marked the end of Iraq's participation in U.S.-backed regional defense arrangements and of Baghdad's close cooperation with Western countries in many fields.

In 1969, a small group of Libyan army officers headed by Muammer Qaddafi overthrew the government of King Idris. I had served until three months before the coup as ambassador to Libya and at the time of the coup was assistant secretary for African affairs in Washington. This coup ended close cooperation with Libya, including the use by the U.S. Air Force of Wheelus Air Base outside of Tripoli.

In 1975, a leftist military group toppled the regime of Haile Selassie of Ethiopia. I had been one of the officials who in earlier years had sensed the uncertain future of the emperor's regime and had sought to persuade the aging ruler to look to the future and plan for his succession. The United States lost a friendly regime and important military communications facilities at Asmara.

In 1979, when I was under secretary of state, I witnessed the overthrow of the shah of Iran and the efforts to find a non-leftist alternative to the rule of Somoza in Nicaragua.

Congressional and press reaction in the United States suggested a feeling of American responsibility for what happened —almost a sense of guilt—in each of these events. People spoke of the United States as having "lost" a country, even when the people of that country could not save it. Such upheavals in other countries have been seen by Americans in the postwar period as an indication of their lack of vigilance or influence, rather than as signs of serious weaknesses in the leadership of a foreign country.

Americans thus personalize their view of governments, leaders, and problems. As stated earlier, they regard friendship as a key factor in the nation's foreign relationships, which gives the appearance of a close U.S. identification with regimes and rulers. Many U.S. diplomats have had the experience of drafting statements for U.S. leaders to be given during a meeting with a foreign head of state. When correct cordiality rather than effusiveness is suggested, the political leaders have disagreed: "The statement is not friendly enough." The result can be a message that conveys to the local population an impression of U.S. support for an unpopular leader in deep trouble.

Political changes in countries where the United States has had major military facilities or strategic involvement have usually ended the relationship and damaged U.S. interests largely because of this impression of support for a previous regime. New leaders have frequently considered the United States a principal adversary either because the United States is slow to resume diplomatic relations with the new regime, is associated with the oppressive acts of the predecessor, or because of suspicion that Washington may seek to reestablish a former regime.

Americans tend to explain political change in terms of inimical external influences and subversion, all part of a deliberate effort by adversaries to outflank the U.S. geopolitical position. The possibility that revolutions basically come from built-up internal grievances is difficult to accept. To be sure, external elements may be involved, but their efforts would likely fail if the society and the regime were strong.

The United States does not live easily with abrupt change; the coup d'état is not part of American tradition. Yet the United States is often an instrument of change. With the establishment by the Congress of the National Endowment for Democracy in 1985, the United States is officially committed, as never before, to promote democratic governments in other countries.

Many who lead coups against oppressive regimes claim inspiration from U.S. history and philosophy. Bitter opponents of authoritarian regimes friendly to the United States have been students returning from an American education who have seen the contrast between the freedoms they observed as students and the reality of their own country.

American communities abroad, by their life style, also have an impact, both favorable and unfavorable. Although individual Americans may build strong personal relationships in a country, wealthier foreigners may be objects of envy and resentment. When Americans introduce new methods in agriculture or education, whether through the private sector or governmental assistance programs, the inadequacy of traditional ways becomes apparent and demands for new social and political policies are generated.

American films and American television, widely viewed abroad, present life styles in sharp contrast to the poverty and oppression that exist in many countries. Such images create pressures for change; at the same time, conservatives in traditional societies regard these American exports as a source of unsettling radical political and social influences. That the United States was seen as the villain in Iran's Islamic revolution was due in part to the deep resentment in conservative Muslim societies against the cultural influences stemming from the West and, in particular, from the United States.

Modern communications have stimulated change in other ways. The impact of the French Revolution was eventually felt throughout Europe—but the immediate effect was confined to Paris. Today, as in the case of Iran, one man living in a village south of Paris could by telephone and tape recorder arouse a whole nation to revolt nearly 3,000 miles away.

The seeds of such change are planted deep and they mature slowly. Pressures originate from many quarters and many factors: population growth, urban migration, disillusionment with leaders, discriminatory educational policies, corruption, excessive living costs, and the absence of institutionalized procedures for leadership succession.

Although some coups may be sudden spur-of-the-moment affairs, many represent a long period of planning by a small, tight group. Coups against established leaders succeed either when there are few who will raise their hands to defend the ruler or when the depth of dissatisfaction is such that the revolutionaries ride the crest of a popular wave. When Qaddafi staged his coup in Libya, no one raised a hand to defend the regime of King Idris, although the king was not a despised ruler. Some did raise a hand to defend the shah of Iran, but the weight of a mass revolution swept away this defense.

In much of the Third World, individual rulers are more important than institutions or constitutions. A smooth succession depends upon the willingness of a ruler to look beyond death. Aging rulers, loath to give up power or to face and prepare for their death, present an open invitation to radical change. Invariably they are reluctant to choose a successor or to give scope to one chosen, because the moment a choice is made, they lose part of their aura and power; those around the throne immediately begin to curry favor with the future, not the past. It is the royal, authoritarian version of the "lame duck."

Radical change is often unexpected and undetected. Leaders may be unknown even to the rulers of a regime and the police apparatus. Muammer Qaddafi of Libya was known to few; his role in the coup became known only several days after the coup itself.

As in Libya, many coups originate in the military. The younger military officers who have revolts in their minds are the very ones who, being nationalistic and often xenophobic, shut themselves off from outsiders. In countries with which the United States has a close military relationship they may be the ones who most resent the dependence created by that relationship. In Iran, the first open revolt against the U.S. military presence was by noncommissioned air force technicians especially trained by the United States.

Although revolts may be led by military officers, they succeed because of a general malaise or dissatisfaction in a country. Economic dislocations created by the pressure to modernize or by sudden new wealth can contribute to such a climate. In most developing countries with stable village societies, poverty in itself may not breed revolt. The exodus of the poor from their villages to urban areas in search of better opportunities, however, can result in mass support for violent change if the economic situation deteriorates further. Increased urbanization results in new social classes, heightened expectations, and profound challenges to value systems and traditional beliefs. These were among the elements leading to the revolution in Iran.

Sudden wealth may also increase the consciousness in a society of the disparity between the rich and the poor. With this awareness often goes a growing public concern with corruption. Official corruption may reach a point where it is beyond even the normal tolerance of a people. The pressures on an Asian or African ruler for favors expected by those surrounding him, supported by long tradition, can be irresistible. King Idris of Libya permitted one family, the Shalhi family, to profit substantially from the negotiation of oil contracts. The widespread knowledge of this was undoubtedly an element in the lack of support for the king at the time of the coup. Few challenge the conclusion that the misuse of relief funds following the Managua earthquake in Nicaragua contributed to the final weakening of Somoza's regime. An Arab merchant sitting next to me on an airplane a few years ago said to me with great assurance, "I can always tell when a coup is about to take place in a country. It is when the side payments to officials on a contract reach over 25 percent."

There are other signs to watch for. A ruler may become so isolated that he is solely dependent upon advisors close to him for a view of events. They are unlikely to give him the truth about local opposition or resentment of his rule. The domination of one ethnic or religious group by another or age-old tensions between groups can become exacerbated in periods of unrest. A taunting intolerance, desires for revenge, and ambitions for power characterize ancient rivalries. The tragic divisions in Lebanon stem from bitter hatred built up among internal family and religious groups; outside forces, whether Palestinian or Israeli, removed what fabric of accord existed.

A vicious cycle of brutal repression can be another cause. To stay in power, a regime may clamp down hard on its citizens. That very act not only weakens the regime's ability to govern, but also adds a measure of vengeance to political change when it comes. Authoritarian regimes live by oppression. As their popularity declines, the oppression grows. They depend more and more on the security services that provide the information and carry out the acts of violence against the population. The ruler is beholden to these services for his survival—or has, at least, been led to believe so.

In another era, the weaknesses of other regimes would have attracted less attention in the United States. The global position of the United States following World War II, however, made it inevitable that American diplomats would be involved in the internal affairs of other countries. In the confrontation with the Soviets around the world, the stability of friendly regimes became vital to global support for U.S. policies, the retention of military facilities, and the maintenance of regional defense alliances. Given these national concerns, the U.S. diplomat has been called upon to detect the seeds of unrest, report them, and look for ways to protect U.S. interests in the event of change. This task requires the mobilization of an embassy to establish relationships with as many elements of a population as possible. The diplomat must evaluate the degree to which pressures for change are building as well as assess the quarters from which a threat to the existing government might come.

In such cases, the diplomat must sift through the traditional barbs and slurs of political rhetoric to detect that degree of genuine bitterness that can presage an explosion. U.S. diplomats in Lebanon were long aware of the deep ethnic and religious differences in that country. It was clear that these could someday explode into dangerous and reciprocating violence. It took only a spark to ignite; it was not possible to predict exactly when that spark would flash.

To assess the possibilities of political change means delving beneath layers of a society often traditionally closed to foreigners. The revolution in Iran could first be detected in the sermons in the Shia mosques. Not only did the shah's regime discourage contact between foreign diplomats and religious leaders, but the mosques were closed to all non-Muslims. The presence of a foreign diplomat, particularly from a non-Muslim country, would probably have been quickly detected.

Cannot the CIA meet this need to "penetrate" these reclusive layers of society? Within some limits, the answer is yes. The priority task of officers of the CIA in friendly countries is, however, generally directed at Soviet, East European, and other adversary elements. Either because of limited resources or, in some cases, agreement with local security services, they do not "target" the local society. When they do, experience suggests that they are no more successful in anticipating trouble through clandestine methods than are the political officers of the embassy who use a more open and direct approach.

When the succession of a ruler has been an issue, American diplomats have been instructed to discuss the future with aging kings and emperors. The subject, as I have said, is not popular. As ambassador in Libya, I raised the succession issue with King Idris and, as a visiting Washington official, with Haile Selassie. With King Idris, a mask came over his face that said quite unmistakably, This subject is out of bounds. Haile Selassie responded by assuring me that all was well; the crown prince would succeed. Yet we knew from other information that he was doing little to support the crown prince, that he was suspicious of him, and that, on one occasion, the emperor had said to close associates that he was not concerned with what would come after his own death.

American diplomats in countries vulnerable to radical change where a clear U.S. interest is at stake can bring their assessment of the situation to the attention of the rulers and officials of the foreign government. They can, beyond that, suggest ways to reduce the threat or to make the regime more acceptable. Suggestions, however, of specific steps that might be taken—reforms, reassuring statements, changes in personnel—are likely to be regarded as unwarranted interference in the ruler's internal affairs. The ruler, quite logically, may feel he knows more about his political environment than does an ambassador. In few cases is the approach fully welcomed.

Seldom if ever will a ruler admit to a foreign diplomat that he is in serious trouble. The reaction is more likely to be that he is being assailed by unfriendly forces—probably communists—and needs more support. His salvation lies not with himself, but with the United States. He may make unrealistic demands for U.S. support.

The diplomat needs to be aware, also, that even an unpopular ruler can turn outside pressures to his benefit by exploiting latent nationalist feelings against external intervention. Such a leader, exploiting the suspicions of fellow countrymen who live in an atmosphere of conspiracy and intrigue, can raise questions about the motive of the foreign government in pressing for reform or change. What is behind this ambassador's effort? Who do the Americans want to put in my place?

Opposition groups in some countries oppose the efforts of foreign diplomats to press reforms upon unpopular regimes. In their view, to do so is merely to seek to perpetuate a basically unacceptable regime through giving the ruler the option of reform.

As in the case of the pursuit of human rights objectives, U.S. diplomatic pressure for reform can be supplemented by signals. A diplomat can increase the number of meetings with known opposition leaders, decline invitations to events of special importance to the ruler, and make equivocal public statements, less warm toward the regime than previous statements. In countries where the U.S. ambassador's actions are closely observed, such signals can begin to plant doubts in a ruler's mind as well as with the local public about the degree of U.S. support. In some cases, these efforts can perhaps make the ruler more receptive to the assessments and suggestions that come from the U.S. embassy.

Signals are important not only to suggest to the ruler a diminished enthusiasm for his rule, but also to suggest to the population that the United States is not inextricably tied to the ruler in power. Until the recent events in the Philippines, the United States had never successfully detached itself from a close identification with a falling, friendly ruler. U.S. actions, even in the case of the Philippines, were clouded by the debate in the United States between those who wished to stay with the ruler to the bitter end and those who would support change, with all of its risks.

To effect such a detachment, a diplomat must have the certainty of support in Washington. When the ruler hears from his embassy in Washington that U.S. administration officials are reiterating their earlier expressions of support, the word of the diplomat on the spot has little force. The U.S. government is not, by its nature, capable of the subtle application of pressure. Such tactics are not, therefore, easy for its diplomats. Diverse opinions within the government, varied channels to a ruler, and the ever-present possibility of leaks disclosing a strategy make exceedingly difficult any broad orchestration of a pattern of pressure for change. In the Philippines, the United States was aided by the traditional relationship with that country as well as a strong opposition movement. Such conditions are not likely to be duplicated in other areas.

Reports of possible unrest or change in a country in which the United States has important interests are not always welcomed by Washington. Much depends on the credibility of the ambassador or the reporting officer. The report's assessment must compete with other information flowing to the decision makers from intelligence sources, the military, business, other capitals, and friends of the beleaguered ruler. Policymakers gain a vested interest in the continuance of a comfortable relationship with a ruler or a regime, a relationship solidified occasionally by the rhetoric of toasts or arrival statements during visits. Perhaps there have been letters from the U.S. president to the ruler indicating an official interest and support. When an ambassador reports that the ruler is in trouble and may not survive, policymakers naturally will seek more optimistic opinions.

How the United States reacts as a government and as a nation inevitably affects the attitudes of its principal allies and other nations in the area. If the U.S. government seems to fail to support a friend, this can cast doubt on U.S. assurances to others. Adversaries, too, take advantage of the circumstances of a coup against a friend of the United States to exploit anti-American feelings in a region.

The United States cannot deal with crises of political change in silence or at leisure. The speed of communications, the debate over different approaches, and the pressure of events make reaction inevitable. Reaction, in turn, can directly affect the events creating the concern. A statement that the United States "no longer supports" a ruler can speed the ruler's fall; a statement of support when all hope has gone can make relations with the successor regime more difficult.

When change does take place, policymakers in Washington must adopt an attitude toward the new regime. Is the change to be welcomed or accepted as an inevitable fact? Are hopes entertained that the process can be reversed? Are statements of support more likely to harm or to help a new regime?

The first decision that must be made is whether to continue diplomatic relations with the new regime. The current United States policy is to "recognize" nations and not governments. The act of continuing relations carries with it no need to pass judgment on the new regime's political acceptability, as Washington was compelled to do in the case of the People's Republic of China. It merely signifies a determination that the new regime is effectively in power and will meet its international obligations. Further decisions will involve the continuation of aid programs, military sales, and trade preferences. If relations with a new regime are controversial, the public debate over these policies will both delay final decisions and lessen the effectiveness of the ultimate policy. Whatever may have been the possibilities of satisfactory relationships between the United States and the Sandinista regime in Nicaragua, they were reduced by the several months of acrimonious congressional debate that preceded decisions on the aid program.

Not all political change has been adverse to U.S. interests. The changes in Indonesia in 1965, in Egypt in 1973, in Portugal in 1974, and in Spain in 1975 are examples. When change is viewed as favorable to U.S. interests, diplomats in the field have often cautioned against effusive statements or assumptions of new policies that may be incorrect or premature. The U.S. government, in such cases, must walk a narrow line between raising unrealistic expectations of support and identifying the new regime too closely with Washington or seeming to be indifferent to the change. Even when a revolution promises a radical departure, not all basic national tendencies will be changed. The Indonesian regime that replaced Sukarno in 1965 did not intend, for example, to depart from the traditional Indonesian stance of non-alignment. The political maneuvering within any country remains within boundaries established by history and tradition.

When regimes are unfriendly to the United States, dissident politicians may approach U.S. diplomats with plans to overthrow the government. As tempting as these offers may be, the wise diplomat will reject them. They could be a trap by the regime in power; they could have little prospect of

success. It is almost certain that approaches such as this—
and the American response —will become known.

The prospect of political change presents diplomats with
special tasks and difficulties. The U.S. political system, the
tendency to look at the world in terms of friendship, and the
view of the world as an arena of East-West conflict complicate
efforts to deal with the weaknesses of societies in which there
are significant U.S. interests. Problems of political change
will, no doubt, continue to bedevil both American policymakers and diplomats.

X

THE TERRORIST THREAT
TO DIPLOMACY

TERRORISM HAS CHANGED the face of diplomacy. American embassies used to present a hospitable front. People entered through open doors. They encountered pleasant receptionists. They waited, when necessary, in attractively decorated rooms. They proceeded on their own to the officer they were visiting. Only in certain traditionally secure areas of an embassy were escorts required. Today the visitor enters through a screen of local guards and a metal detector. In the embassy itself, the visitor faces a U.S. Marine guard through a thick glass shield and must present identification. Escorts are required for those entering any part of the embassy.

The life of the individual diplomat has changed, too. The ambassador moves about in an armored limousine and, in most cases, with a local guard in the front seat. Routes to and from the office are varied each day. Limousines are wired with transmitters that immediately reveal to monitors in the embassy the occurrence of anything unusual in the limousine.

As this is being written, a congressionally mandated report has recommended the total rebuilding of U.S. missions abroad at a cost of $1.4 billion. Inevitably this will mean, even if only partially implemented, an even more inhospitable face to the outside world and less freedom of movement for U.S. diplomats. This greater concern over security is understandable and has been heightened by the events in the 1980s in which U.S. embassies were attacked in Beirut and Kuwait, further American hostages were taken, and individual Americans were the victims of attacks in Europe and Central America.

Much of the impetus to new measures has been created by an administration and a Congress concerned not only with the lives of the diplomats, but also with the image of a major nation being continually attacked and humiliated by forces of clearly inferior power. It is symbolic of the courage of American diplomats that no crisis was created by their refusal to serve under the dangerous conditions prevailing in some areas. There is, in fact, no want of volunteers to serve in such places. Bearing this burden as it does, the United States must balance the threat against diplomats with the normal conduct of diplomacy. Improved security is clearly essential, not only because of terrorism, but also because of efforts of other powers to penetrate our embassies through agents and by electronic means.

Forty years ago there was little security. For the first few years of our embassy in Pakistan, the guards were entirely local. These *chokadars*, as they were called, were accustomed to sleeping through the night but had trained themselves to rise up or cough at intervals so possible intruders knew of their presence. Even in 1948, this was not acceptable to a U.S. security officer. He required that they stay awake all night. One evening he went to inspect and found that they were awake—but in order to remain so, they had, out of their meager wages, hired a group of musicians to play for them.

Through the intervening years Marine guards, assigned primarily to protect doeuments and cryptography, have been a standard feature of U.S. embassies and major consular officers. Access to areas of possible sensitivity has increasingly been limited. Beginning in the 1960s, ambassadors in areas of particular threat have been provided with bodyguards, usually from the host country's security services. The U.S. ambassador to the Argentine, during the height of that country's terrorist problem, went everywhere with cars of armed police ahead and behind his limousine.

The security problem has been exacerbated because terrorism is no longer confined to the area in which it breeds. With modern transportation and links among terrorist organizations, Middle East terrorists can carry out attacks in Europe, Asia, whatever circumstances may permit. Terrorists are more sophisiticated and, at the same time, more daring. Host governments, whose basic responsibility it is to protect diplomats, are less and less capable of doing so. In some cases, as in Iran and Syria, government agencies are themselves involved with the terrorists.

Perhaps gravest of all is the threat to the established convention of diplomatic immunity. As governments have become involved either in condoning or facilitating acts of terror, they have used the cover of diplomatic pouches, diplomatic communications, and immune personnel to transport explosives and weapons and to arrange acts of violence. James Reston addressed this in a column in the *New York Times* (Oct. 13, 1985):

> But in some parts of the world, an ambassador is sent abroad to murder for his country, and when he is found out, is merely expelled and then honored as a hero when he gets home.
> What can be done about all this is hard to tell. There has to be privacy and some kind of immunity for civilized embassies and their servants, but not immunity for murder. . . .

Despite the terrorist threat, if diplomats are still to be effective, they cannot avoid risks. The diplomat cannot be completely protected at a national day reception at another embassy, in the local government office where business must be transacted, or in transit to and from the residence. Terrorism, in the form of acts of violence that threaten the lives and property of diplomats, is not new. Americans are not the only victims. There is, for example, the series of assassinations of Turkish diplomats by Armenian extremists. The problem has been a threat to the diplomacy of many nations, including the United States, for many years.

Three close friends of mine, John Gordon Mein, ambassador to Guatemala in 1968, Frank Meloy, ambassador to Lebanon in 1976, and Rodger Davies, U.S. ambassador to Cyprus in 1974, were gunned down in the course of their duties. I was the object of a death threat from a Palestinian group when I was ambassador to Libya in 1967. As Assistant Secretary of State for African Affairs in 1973, I was in the State Department Operations Center throughout the tragic unfolding of the kidnapping and murder of our ambassador to the Sudan, Cleo Noel, and his deputy, Curt Moore. We have all heard about plots against other colleagues that were either frustrated or failed to come off. I was one of those who spent many sleepless nights wondering how we could gain the release of the 57 U.S. hostages, many of them friends, held in Iran from 1979 to 1981.

In the lobby of the State Department in Washington are two plaques memorializing those in the U.S. diplomatic service who died in the line of duty. The first plaque took 187 years to be filled. The second plaque is almost filled after 18 years, and it excludes—unlike the first—those who died of disease and natural disasters.

Americans, deeply disturbed by the general threat of worldwide terrorism ask, "Why Americans? Why are the Soviets never the victims?" The answer is that Americans are involved in the areas that create today's conspicuous terrorist acts. The Soviets are victims in regions such as Central Asia and Afghanistan where they are identified as supporting the oppressor. The outside world knows relatively little of this terrorism. In the regions where the United States faces the major terrorist threats, the Soviet Union has never held the preeminent position. Those who are in the camps and regions that breed terrorism do not see the Soviets as their enemy.

The apparent immunity of the Russians may in part be because they pay greater attention to security and generate a greater fear of retaliation. But it is also because they are not seen to be involved, as is the United States, in the turmoil of troubled regions such as the Middle East.

U.S. diplomats, often the victims of terrorism, may understand better than people at home why Americans are so often the target. Earlier chapters have suggested some of the many reasons why individuals may harbor bitter sentiments against the United States: envy of American wealth and power, the impact of American ways on traditional cultures, unfulfilled expectations of U.S. support, disinformation by adversaries, and unpopular regional policies, particularly in southern Africa, Central America, and the Middle East.

The people of many countries have come, over the years, to identify the United States with hated regimes or external adversaries. Those who hesitate to attack their own governments for fear of a strong reaction may attack a U.S. embassy instead. The mob that attacked the U.S. information office in Baghdad in 1952 was protesting a treaty between the United Kingdom and Iraq in which the United States played no part. But the popular belief was that the United States was clearly the major power in the area; no moves would be made without its concurrence.

Twenty years ago an Arab friend returned from a visit to the Palestine refugee camps in Lebanon. He was clearly shocked at what he had seen. He told me that the camps were creating a generation of alienated and frustrated youth that would at some time in the future make a hell of the Middle East. "We will all be their victims," he said. He left unsaid that the United States would be one of the targets of their frustration.

Although terrorism built on the frustrations in the Middle East may be fanatical, it is not insane. To those who take such actions, there is a purpose. It springs from antipathies so deep that men and women will undertake suicidal attacks. The willingness of someone to risk life to kill or harass an American is based on more than hatred. But the hatred feeds the atmosphere from which individuals are coerced or recruited into terrorist acts. The architect of the act may not run the risk; he or she will have the capacity to persuade, force, or embolden others to do the deed. The architect's motive may not even be to strike at the Americans. Acts by Arab terrorists against Americans and other foreigners may be designed to sabotage the peace efforts of moderate Arabs identified with the United States. In the Middle East, striking at an American is a convenient means of accomplishing other mischief.

The environment for terrorist acts against the United States is not unique to the Middle East. In scattered pockets around the world in the postwar years, conditions have bred generations who believe that the United States stands in the way of their aspirations toward political power or a better life. Elders teach their young to hate the nation they believe supports their immediate oppressor. This has been true in the villages of Iran, in the hinterland of Central America, and in the refugee camps of Lebanon. When such youth reach the age of action and see so little future they long to strike at this "enemy."

Moderate governments often remain quiet in the face of terrorism. They recognize the latent sympathy in their own populations for the cause promoted by the terrorist; they understand, also, the risk to them of trying to apprehend or punish terrorists. In the Middle East, leaders who would seek peace with Israel or oppose extremist acts recall vividly the many victims of terrorism, from King Abdullah of Jordan to Anwar Sadat of Egypt.

It is facile to suggest that the resentment that breeds such attacks comes primarily from the policies of a U.S. administration. The strong U.S. support for Israel in the Middle East, for the shah and his excesses in Iran, or for Somoza in

Nicaragua are wellsprings, however, of truly anti-American sentiment. But there are numerous other sources of resentment that can lead to acts against Americans.

In the divided Arab world, where conspiracy is a tradition, one side sees Washington's hand in the machinations of its adversaries. Christian groups see the United States supporting their Christian rivals. Muslims see the Americans supporting Christians. The breakup of Lebanon and the anarchy of Beirut provide the perfect settings for terrorist acts that spring from such resentments.

Identifying the sources of terrorism is not difficult; creating a national policy to deal with terrorism is. It is frequently suggested that the United States could reduce its vulnerability to terrorism from the Middle East by a change in policies that are seen throughout the region as favoring Israel in the Arab-Israel conflict. U.S. administrations will undoubtedly continue to seek ways to lessen the tensions in the Middle East, but it is unlikely that any U.S. government would risk appearing to change policies under the threat of terrorism. Although U.S. policies have varied in their degree of balance, the commitment to Israel is strong; it is difficult to imagine a change that would satisfy the more extreme Palestinian and Shia factions. U.S. vulnerability in the region would be lessened if Arab governments were prepared to cooperate with the United States and with each other in the prevention of terrorist acts. To do so, the position of the United States would need to move closer to a recognition of the Palestinian cause than seems possible today. Moreover, the deep divisions in the Arab world over the Palestinian issue would need to be bridged. The possibilities of lessening the threat to the United States through a fundamental change in the Arab perception of U.S. policy, therefore, seem remote. The United States will need to meet the problem of terrorism in other ways.

Negotiating with terrorists in some circumstances is a possibility. The United States has traditionally held to a policy of not negotiating with terrorists. In the view of some who support this policy, the lives of potential victims are secondary to preserving U.S. honor and to avoiding the establishment of a precedent that might encourage further terrorist acts. Although these are laudable bases for a policy, too rigid a declared position prevents the flexibility that may be necessary in dealing effectively with terrorist cases and may, at times, put lives at risk. A case can be made, on the basis of the timing of events, that President Nixon's statement in a press conference while Ambassador Noel and Curt Moore were being held in Khartoum that "we will not pay blackmail"* was a factor in the decision of the kidnappers to kill Noel and Moore. President Reagan's capacity to deal with the hostage problem was hindered by his strong rhetoric at the beginning of his term about not dealing with terrorists.

In some areas of potential danger, a U.S. diplomat has, in the past, been able to find intermediaries through whom approaches could be made to discourage terrorism or to effect the release of hostages. If one is to discourage or resolve terrorist actions, some communication is obviously necessary. To be effective, an intermediary must be credible to the terrorists and have the capacity to convince them in some fashion either that the demands will not be met or that it is not otherwise in their interests to continue the acts of violence.

In effect, this is what the Algerian government did in its role as intermediary between the United States and Iran during the hostage crisis in 1980. The Algerians helped convince the Iranians that some of their demands were not realistic in the light of the laws and institutions of the United States; the insistence upon the return of the shah's assets was one such demand. As the Algerian ambassador to the United States, who was one of the mediating team, explained to me, "We were not actually mediators. We were conducting seminars in each capital to educate the other side on the realistic

*New York Times, Mar. 3, 1973.

limits of negotiation." In the Iran case, pressure was applied through diplomatic and economic sanctions. The Iranian recognition of its isolation was one factor that led ultimately to the decision to release the hostages. This possibility was made easier because, unlike later Middle East hostage cases, a recognized government ultimately took responsibility for the hostages.

In Lebanon in the 1970s, before the total collapse of that country, the United States was able to deal secretly, through intermediaries, with members of the Palestine Liberation Organization to assure the safety of U.S. diplomats in the area. This possibility ended with the elimination of the PLO presence in Lebanon in 1984. The unknown or remote terrorists of today are largely beyond the reach of the kind of intermediaries the United States once used. Washington often does not know with any certainty what person or group lies behind attacks.

Demands of such terrorists have in some instances become impossible to meet. No U.S. administration, for example, would be likely to agree to the condition posed by the captors of the American hostages in Lebanon in 1986 that Washington pressure the Kuwaiti government to release the terrorists who had fire-bombed the American embassy in that country.

The U.S. government has held to a policy of not paying ransom under any circumstances. The outcry at the time of the reported exchange of arms for Iran for hostages in 1986 suggests that the public supports this position. In at least one case of a kidnapping of a Peace Corps volunteer in Latin America, ransom was arranged through a member of Congress without the participation of the executive branch. In another, an American diplomat permitted the embassy to be used for a discussion of ransom with terrorists. This type of official involvement, however, has been rare.

Uncertainty can be a useful tactic in dealing with terrorists who may have an exaggerated idea of the capacity of the United States, or any other country, either to rescue victims or to retaliate effectively. When the hostages were seized in Iran in November 1979, the Carter administration tried to send a presidential message to the Ayatollah Khomeini through a special envoy, former Attorney General Ramsey Clark. Before that attempt, Khomeini could not have known how the United States would react; the early message from President Carter may have given him the impression that the U.S. capacity to respond in some more vigorous way was less than he had believed. A strategy of calculated risk by refusing any communication until the hostages had been released was never tried.

In the aftermath of a terrorist act, many Americans favor military retaliation. As momentarily satisfying as this may be to the national psyche, the problems are manifold in terms of identifying the terrorists, mobilizing opinion, and pinpointing the target. The risk is high that retaliating against the type of terrorists that exist in today's world may only kill innocent victims and perpetuate a cycle of violence. As this is written the full effects of the U.S. military attack on Libya in April 1986 are still being assessed.

No less controversial than the question of how to deal with terrorists is the matter of affording publicity to terrorist acts. The terrorist today has a channel through which he can speak to the world in the Western media. After each terrorist incident, a debate ensues in the United States over whether such persons should be given this opportunity. Many Americans would place restrictions on the degree to which television in particular gives a voice to the terrorist. It is difficult to see how First Amendment freedoms can be preserved and, at the same time, official limitations placed on as prominent a story as that of a terrorist act. At times, the press has voluntarily withheld news involving terrorist acts. In some circumstances, however, publicity may have reduced the risk to hostages. In each case, difficult judgments about news coverage must be made; in a democracy, those judgments will be made largely by editors and news directors, not by government officials.

This chapter has dwelt on the threat of terrorism for the U.S. diplomat, particularly in the Middle East. The threat to Americans in the rest of the world is less. Through most of the world, the United States continues to be deeply respected and looked up to as a leader. This is particularly true in those areas that have had the closest experiences with the Soviet Union. That being said, Americans should not be surprised when free, ebullient, and often provocative actions and the pursuit of policies that reflect the nation's global responsibilities, diversity, and democracy should, in some areas, arouse deep currents of hatred that cannot be fully controlled.

American diplomats are not foolhardy. They are only too well aware of their vulnerability. They accept the fact that in some unsettled areas of the world, such as the Middle East, fanatical terrorists, reacting to local perceptions of U.S.policies, have declared war on the U.S. presence; diplomats are among the targets. They realize that a great country cannot alter policies under the pressure of violent acts. There must be adequate prudent protection, however, for those in such circumstances.

The U.S. diplomat recognizes another factor as well. The diplomatic mission cannot be performed inside a fortress. The very same Congress and public that support the strong emphasis on counterterrorist activity also want U.S. embassies abroad to be aware of trends in areas of conflict where our interests are at stake and to play a role in influencing governments and peoples. To accomplish these tasks, there must be a balance between diplomacy and security.

Whatever measures may be taken to enhance embassy security, an element of risk to diplomats will remain. To do their job, they must go beyond the barriers, get out of their limousines, and attend events on other premises. Every appropriate precaution can be taken in planning schedules and in accepting protection, but it is unwise to expect that Americans can avoid further sacrifice if the United States is to remain diplomatically effective.

There is a tendency in the United States, when extraordinary measures are taken to meet a threat, to regard any further disasters as failures. In the world of today's diplomacy, Americans should do all they can, but they cannot totally encase their representatives in armor plate and effectively conduct the diplomacy required of a great nation.

XI

✑

THE ROLE OF INTELLIGENCE

No PART OF OFFICIAL activity abroad illustrates more clearly the dilemma of an open society in pursuit of effective diplomacy than the role of clandestine intelligence. Uneasy with secrets yet fascinated by them, Americans approach intelligence with romantic expectations. At the same time they are suspicious and skeptical about the art.

Emerging into the status of a world power after World War II, the United States recognized with some reluctance the need for a permanent intelligence capacity. That capacity was to embrace both the clandestine collection of intelligence and the ability to undertake covert political and paramilitary action. The Soviet Union was continuing to build its strength in these fields. Washington saw the need to "fight fire with fire." The intelligence function became part of the U.S. diplomatic apparatus.

Americans want their nation to be able to predict and influence events around the world. Surprises, whether in political change, strategic threats, or economic disasters, can affect the United States severely. Americans therefore expect U.S. intelligence not only to know what may happen, but also,

136

at times, to make it happen or to prevent its happening. Their expectations embrace both the gathering of information and the launching of covert actions.

In the gathering of information, Americans have been disappointed that the U.S. intelligence network appears to have failed. They ask, for example: Why did we not know in advanceof the plans to bomb the embassy in Beirut (in 1984) or, later, the Marines' barracks? We had an embassy and, presumably, intelligence operatives. Or did we? Did someone in the government have the information and not pass it along? Was it passed along and not used? Did high officials ignore it?

In their expectations, Americans are in fact putting their trust in a complex and imperfect process. Individual mistakes in the gathering and evaluation of intelligence have undoubtedly been made, yet the real problems may lie elsewhere: in the process of gathering intelligence, in the complexity of the intelligence bureaucracy, and in the final use of information by the policymakers.

Those conditioned by the novels of Ian Fleming are surprised and somewhat disappointed to find that the bulk of intelligence activity is not gadget ridden, sexually stimulating, or violently dangerous. Much intelligence is the hard work of perusing documents, studying photographs, reviewing endless files, or seeking out individuals with personal vulnerabilities that will turn them to espionage. Information rarely comes by magic. Foreigners can only acquire information that others will give them or which can be obtained through technology.

Intelligence is an intensely human process. Although technological developments in satellite photography and electronic surveillance have enhanced the nation's capacity to "look in and listen in," the ultimate dependence is on the human source. A photograph can show tanks on the ground; only a human source can tell who is inside and where they are going. The role of intelligence in embassies is important because it concentrates on the development of human sources.

A clandestine service can penetrate another society primarily by finding those disenchanted persons with serious problems who are open to inducements of money or future exile. In a tight, authoritarian society, however, the pressures against such defection are intense. They are equally so in many military establishments; the risk of being charged with treason is a strong deterrent to cooperation with outsiders. In any society, the process of developing such agents can take years.

The products of the intelligence process are often fragmentary. The source who can provide a complete blueprint of a Kremlin decision or a forthcoming coup is rare indeed. What a policy officer in Washington is more likely to receive is a snippet: "A source of known reliability told X that the prime minister is likely to resign tomorrow."

The rules of the intelligence community do not permit the person receiving the information in most cases to know the source. The intelligence officer's assessment of the reliability of the source must be taken on faith. Rarely, too, do the reports suggest the motive for the giving of the information. Is it someone who, by telling the United States that the prime minister is likely to resign, hopes that this will hasten the act? Is it someone who wants to alert the United States in the hope they will discourage the act?

I was once given a report that purported to be a verbatim account of a cabinet meeting in a foreign country. The account differed from information from persons who had been present at the meeting. I asked the intelligence officer whether this was based on a recording of the meeting or a memorandum of the meeting prepared by an aide to one of the ministers. It was the latter. It then became clear that the information was inaccurate because the aide, in his report, wanted to portray the proceedings in a way favorable to his boss.

In the United States, efforts to sift significant information out of imprecise raw material are compounded by the complexity of the intelligence bureaucracy. At any given time, a huge volume of information is flowing into Washington from around the world through many channels—the ambassadors and political officers of the embassies, the CIA, the Defense Intelligence Agency, the operatives of the separate armed services agencies, the National Security Agency, and, where domestic aspects are involved, the FBI.

The preferred "cover" for U.S. intelligence personnel is within a U.S. embassy, although officers may also be assigned to military establishments or, in rare cases, to private firms abroad. Somewhere in most U.S. embassies, restricted enclaves house the representatives of the intelligence community.

Reporting is also a major responsibility of the ambassador and the regular embassy staff. There will, however, always be information that is vital and that is not available through open methods. That fact dictates that this nation must be served, as are other nations, by an effective clandestine intelligence network. Mystique and misinformation surrounds the tasks of these intelligence units. Some officials in Washington, particularly in the higher echelons, place a special value on clandestine reporting, believing that it may give a more accurate picture of the conditions in a nation than the more overt reporting of the regular embassy personnel. Others, both in Washington and among foreigners abroad, credit "the Agency" with a capacity for collection and reporting well beyond its means or intentions. As an ambassador, I have frequently had U.S. official visitors who will say in a hushed and somewhat reverent voice, after I have briefed them on a problem, "That is all very interesting, but what do the Agency people say?"

Although in many friendly foreign countries political leaders suspect the CIA of spying on them, in general the CIA is charged primarily with following the activities of Soviet and satellite embassies in that country. The activities of Cuba and Libya have been added in recent years. CIA personnel pay attention to the internal politics of the country of assignment only if internal developments in that country are of special significance to the United States. Nevertheless, whatever the assigned tasks of a CIA station, their active personnel will move around the city and the country and inevitably will develop information on local conditions. Sometimes foreign sources will seek them out to volunteer information. The impression that U.S. intelligence officers have an interest in local conditions is difficult to avoid.

U.S. intelligence organizations, each with its own channel to Washington, seek to develop networks of agents abroad. Each has funds to further its objectives. The activities of these agencies inevitably create internal jealousies and rivalries with the overt political officers of the embassy. Information and access to a secret source are elements of power, whether in a diplomatic mission or in an executive department in Washington. The ambassador has the responsibility to lessen these internal tensions.

This multiple pursuit of sources sometimes bemuses and bewilders foreigners. The practice also provides an opportunity for foreign sources to exploit the competition and play one source off against another. While some sources are elusive others will court as many of the members of the U.S. mission as they can. Some cling to the belief that the CIA has greater access to the key decision makers in Washington than the State Department officers in the embassy. Ambassadors have the authority to restrict access to the head of government and to the foreign minister, but they cannot totally eliminate the confusion over the multiple efforts of active intelligence officers.

The presence of competing intelligence agencies within an embassy means, often, that in a time of crisis there is a rush to be first to Washington with critical information. The agency is "one up" that is ahead in reporting to a senior official at the White House a critical bit of intelligence. Because the CIA controls the worldwide diplomatic communications network, that agency is often assumed to be a foregone winner in this competition. My own experience suggests that the agency does have the advantage of a few minutes' lead in the transmission of critical information, but I have not known of any instances where significant messages of other agencies have been purposely delayed by CIA communications personnel in order to give CIA a bureaucratic advantage.

The various agencies within an embassy do have different perspectives on a given piece of information. CIA personnel may paint the darkest picture to protect themselves against any failure to predict a dire event. The defense attache wants to insure that the military component of a problem is given sufficient weight. The foreign service officers will be cautious in their predictions, sensitive to possible leaks that may damage diplomatic relations.

These different approaches become relevant when the information reaches Washington. The process of a joint assessment is then undertaken; like most activities in the American system, this is a political process. The various special interests of the participating agencies come into play. Each intelligence element then tends to support its own source and its own corresponding view of events. Valuable time is lost in getting information to the policymaker through bureaucratic and sometimes political battles over assessments. The time required can sometimes outlast the crisis. The Carter administration was unable to reach an agreed intelligence assessment on the crisis situation in Iran at the time of the fall of the shah. The Reagan administration did not wait for an agreed assessment before proceeding with its approaches to Iran.

Much of the information coming into Washington will consist of rumor, reports from unevaluated sources, intercepted communications, and data from complicated electronic and photographic equipment requiring processing, interpretation, and collateral confirmation. In times of stress, the flow will be supplemented by unevaluated material from those who want to appear informed or make mischief, or are looking for money. Nevertheless, each item must be looked at and evaluated.

Although every effort is made to alert those in crisis areas to relevant intelligence, information relating to one crisis area may come from far away. Only a portion of the total information may be available to officials on the spot or in Washington in time for them to act.

Even in cases of reliable information coming, for example, through intercepted communications, the meaning is not always clear. Conversations can be cryptic, using "doubletalk" and subject to more than one interpretation. Items that are cryptic or unclear when first received may, in the light of more information, have actually foretold events; the later review of such items leads to the impression that officials were, or should have been, informed in advance—when, in fact, the meaning at the time may not have been apparent.

The intelligence analyst in Washington tends to put the greatest credence on known, traditional sources. But, as time passes, and especially in areas of upheaval such as Lebanon, previously available sources may disappear or be of little value in changed political circumstances. The Palestinian and Lebanese officials with which embassies and intelligence agencies once dealt in the Middle East have now lost touch or have departed. The task of penetrating shadowy new sources, particularly in the realm of terrorism, carries more risk and is less certain of results. The task of evaluating becomes even more tenuous.

Given the amount of information received by the United States, a case can be made that almost any event was foreshadowed by someone. That, however, is not the important question. What is meaningful is whether accurate information was sifted, assessed, received in time, and believed by those with the capacity to act and whether there existed, for them, feasible courses of action.

When an intelligence report does go forward, even if it represents the consensus of the intelligence community, it will encounter the commitment of the president and an administration to a given policy, an awareness of congressional attitudes, allied points of view, and public perceptions. As has been stated elsewhere, political leaders whose political success is associated with a given policy prefer information that supports the policy. Other sources are sought that may give a more acceptable view. The public, congressional, and, possibly, allied views may make a change in direction impossible. One need only look at the length of time required for a change in China policy, the move to end the Vietnam War, or the recognition of serious problems in Iran. In each case, reporting from embassies abroad had suggested weaknesses in the premises of policy—reporting that could not be fully accepted because other factors determined whether policies would change. A complex, highly political government such as that of the United States cannot easily or quickly shift policies toward other countries whatever the findings of intelligence may be.

If intelligence suggests that circumstances do not support a policy, Americans ask why the circumstances cannot be changed through U.S. covert action. In each administration there are those, frustrated by the inability of the U.S. to control events, who possess an often unrealistic if not romantic faith in the capacity of U.S. intelligence agencies to manipulate situations in other countries. I have seen this particularly in political figures who enter the government without a profound knowledge of other countries and other societies. In some, an almost childlike belief exists that if the United States will just "unleash the Agency" the nation can solve some of the pesky problems that bedevil it around the world. The attitude springs not only from an incomplete knowledge of the capacity of our intelligence agencies, but from a lack of awareness of the difficulty of covert action in another country by a democratic society.

Advocates of covert action by the United States argue that the Soviet Union appears to "get away" with manipulating other societies. Without pausing to consider whether the United States can or should duplicate the degree of subversion and discipline that marks many leftist guerrilla movements, Americans ask why the United States cannot do the same. Those already inclined toward covert action are sometimes swayed by a persuasive foreigner in exile or dissident politician who suggests that with some money and outside help changes can be wrought in policies or regimes. In fairness to the professional intelligence officers, some of the least feasible and more risky ideas have been generated, not in the CIA, but in other areas of the executive branch.

Disciplined professional experts who, if they are aware of such plans, express their reservations in closed meetings are often not in a position to challenge effectively the determination of higher level officials to proceed. Ambassadors abroad who may or may not be aware of plans for covert action in their area may have even less influence. In some cases, only the congressional oversight committees ask the questions regarding feasibility and risk that are discouraged in the executive branch.

The U.S. record of successes in covert action is not impressive. Neither is the capacity of Washington to keep covert action truly covert. Actions in Iran and Guatemala many years ago were considered successful, although from the hindsight of history this is less clear. The case of the contras in Nicaragua demonstrates how difficult it is to keep any large scale covert action secret, especially in the absence of a broad domestic consensus in support of the action.

Agents of the United States are often, as in the case of the Nicaraguan contras, the prime movers in stimulating and forming the movements. Especially in Latin America, when the U.S. role is revealed, the credibility of the movement suffers. The Americans mounting such large scale paramilitary operations on foreign soil were naive to believe that the dominant role of the United States would not be revealed by at least one of the several thousand people involved.

In its covert action the United States seems destined to depend on those identified with a previous, discredited regime, whose prime motivation may be to recover wealth and authoritarian political power. Such persons lack credibility as well as the capacity to direct a cohesive and disciplined movement. Their association with the United States, certain to be revealed, further damages their credentials. American officials who defend support for covert action in such cases assert that the regime in place, such as the Sandinistas in Nicaragua, is worse than what went before. That may be so, but unless the United States has an alternative that can gain broad national support, covert efforts will be in vain.

The Nicaraguan situation is in contrast to that in Afghanistan where the resistance fighters, even though divided, act on their own initiative and have credibility among the population. Further, support for the Afghan resistance has broad approval within the United States.

Successful covert action requires a knowledge of another society that Americans seldom possess. Despite their diversity, Americans seem to have difficulty truly understanding other countries. To attempt to manipulate the politics of another nation requires the most sophisticated knowledge of its power structure, its culture, its personalities, and its economy, as well as the region around it. Few outsiders, including the KGB, possess that kind of insight. The United States, in particular, with its frequent changes in intelligence leadership and the innate difficulty of preserving secrecy is unsuited for such actions. Proposals hastily drawn under the pressures of short term challenges to U.S. policies are not likely to be successful.

Many U.S. diplomats have been troubled by the propensity toward covert action in situations where secrecy and success are highly doubtful. The United States encourages others to join and risk their lives for a cause the United States may not be prepared fully to support; many a foreign service officer has had to explain failures and to try to help those committed to the United States and stranded by the collapse of a covert action. When such an action is undertaken on the basis of faulty assumptions, the only effect may be to give to America's adversaries a rationale for greater intervention.

The reputation of the CIA was badly distorted, no doubt, by revelations during the 1960s of proposals found in the agency's files, many of which were never seriously considered. To many in the United States and abroad, they were treated as fact. These revelations and the known propensity of some U.S. leaders to consider covert action have added to the myth.

The United States clearly needs an effective, sophisticated, intelligence gathering capacity. There is a real doubt whether the United States can sustain a capacity for covert political action, particularly on a large scale and incorporating paramilitary actions. Successes have been few. For those successes, Americans have paid a price in reduced credibility and an international paranoia about the CIA.

The size and strength of the United States probably would have bred such a paranoia about American involvement in the internal affairs of other nations even if the CIA did not exist. The peoples of the newly independent world believe strongly that major powers have the influence to manipulate events in their countries and that they use that influence. There are those abroad who resent the alleged activities of the CIA. Others count on such activities and want them to be in support of their side. Unsuccessful attempts at covert action make it both difficult to defend the charges of America's adversaries and to encourage its friends.

The intelligence factor is and will remain a part of the United States diplomatic presence. To the extent it works closely to provide U.S. government leaders with reliable information on conditions relating to our major interests, it will continue to be indispensable. To the extent it submits to romantic and clumsy attempts to manipulate other societies, it will harm the very interests it is designed to protect.

XII

𝓟

DIPLOMATS AND THE MILITARY

PARADOXICALLY, THE UNITED STATES—a nation that sees itself as a guardian of the peace—does much to create in other nations an image of a trigger-happy giant and occasional bully. Diplomacy and military action are often presented as contrasting approaches to international problems. In fact, in the United States and most major powers, diplomacy and the capacity to use force are seen as complementary. This chapter will discuss the links that exist between diplomats and representatives of the armed forces as well as some of the problems the United States faces in using force to support diplomacy.

Any treatise on diplomacy should also give attention to the diplomacy of arms control. I had, in my career, only peripheral exposure to this field, but enough to recognize both its great significance and its extreme complexity. Others much closer to this realm of diplomacy have written clearly and authoritatively on it. The basic elements of negotiation, sensitivity to other societies, and deft reporting that are essential to all forms of diplomacy apply particularly to efforts to reach agreements on arms control. As in other areas of U.S. diplomatic activity, the diplomat dealing with negotiations

147

on nuclear and conventional arms is on the short leash of U.S. domestic politics. Negotiators are lost who do not understand the deep divisions within the American body politic over whether to negotiate with the Soviets and whether those negotiations should be merely for the purpose of pleasing our allies, or whether genuine accords limiting and reducing weapons are possible.

Activity on arms control is generally confined to specialized negotiating fora. The military affairs agenda of the Department of State and U.S. embassies abroad includes another range of military subjects: the negotiating and monitoring of military facilities agreements, the health of security alliances, obtaining foreign access for U.S. forces, and the overseeing of military assistance programs. Such programs for the United States, as well as for the Soviet Union, France, Israel, and others, are important means of solidifying and maintaining international relationships with other countries. The sale of military equipment is both a major export and another means of establishing close links with strategically important nations abroad. U.S. embassies have a role in the monitoring of such sales.

The decades since World War II have seen an improvement in the relationship between diplomats and the military, both at the Washington level and in the field. The practice of assigning foreign service and military officers together in senior training courses such as the National Defense University and the Executive Seminar of the Department of State has strengthened the relationship. Establishing the office of the Assistant Secretary for International Security Affairs in the Defense Department as a point of liaison with the State Department has also helped.

Nevertheless, inevitable differences of perspective exist. The diplomat traditionally is looking at the nuances of foreign societies, at the prospects for the resolution of conflict. The military officer is action oriented, trained, and committed to look at the contingencies of conflict. Overseas, the U.S. military officer largely associates with foreign military counterparts who have the same perspective and who frequently share a suspicion of civilian political leaders and diplomats. But like all generalizations, this one has its exceptions. At the higher echelons of the U.S. military, an attitude of caution exists that sometimes places restraints on action-minded civilians. I have frequently been in meetings in the Situation Room of the White House when the representative of the Joint Chiefs of Staff opposed the use of force in support of a diplomatic objective. The military officers, who had to supply the troops and the supporting logistics, often found the proposals of civilians unrealistic. On occasions, also, they expressed doubt about the degree of public support for an operation; they did not want, after Vietnam, to fight another unpopular war.

I was a student at the National War College, a part of the National Defense University, in 1959. The Korean War was still a matter of intense debate. An army colonel who had been sitting in Korea for several years unloaded his feelings one day in a class:

"If it had not been for the chicken-livered State Department that didn't want us to bomb the Chinese across the Yalu River, the outcome might have been quite different."

Another army colonel stood up. "You're wrong," he said. "The problem was not with the State Department. I was on the staff of the Joint Chiefs at that time. The decision not to bomb north of the Yalu was made on military grounds, because we did not want to risk the security of our rear bases in Japan."

Under some circumstances, the military must submit— even if reluctantly—to the authority of diplomats. I was ambassador to Libya during the 1967 Arab-Israeli war. Libya was not directly involved, but the country nevertheless reacted strongly to the Arab defeat and blamed the United States. As ambassador, I felt it prudent to shut down, for a time, the operations of the Wheelus U.S. Air Force Base near

Tripoli. These operations were conspicuous because the F-4 jets, taking off for the nearby bombing range, flew directly over the city. The air force was unhappy about my decision, but I assured them that, ultimately, we could restore operations. A U.S. Air Force general was sent from headquarters in Germany to work with me. At my suggestion, we began a program of limited flights. Two planes would take off one day, four the next. I would then await reactions locally before authorizing further flights. The plan worked, and, ultimately, the base was back in full operation.

Later I learned that, in the midst of this effort, the general had received a sharp message from his headquarters asking why he was permitting the ambassador to "run air force operations." He held his reply until operations had largely been restored, then cabled, "I can't argue with success."

As the Wheelus example illustrates, American diplomats are frequently involved in the efforts to obtain, retain, and assure the use of military facilities abroad. Such facilities are required in support of U.S. strategic plans and to make possible the use of U.S. forces for regional contingencies. The military effort to free the hostages in Iran in 1980 became possible only after the successful negotiation of rights to airfields in nearby Oman.

Embassies also seek rights for maneuvers, ships' visits, and other activities of importance to the U.S. military. Facilities and rights are established in part by alliances such as NATO, in part through separate arrangements with individual states. Such tasks are frequently complicated because the objectives of the foreign nation and those of the United States regarding the arrangements are different.

Some foreign leaders cooperate with the United States in military arrangements because they assume that the United States will come to their aid, militarily, if they are threatened either internally or externally. This impression is created in part by messages in support of a request for base rights that often express the strong interest of the United States in the "continued independence and territorial integrity" of the country involved. This statement can only suggest to a ruler who has a modicum of faith in the United States that Washington means what it says—that U.S. forces would respond to any threat to the country. The United States has yet to use military force to save a base or a ruler who has granted such rights. In Libya under King Idris, there was nothing in the base agreements that suggested the United States would come to the defense of Libya. Wheelus was a training base, not a combat base. Genuine doubt existed, particularly in the years of Vietnam, that Congress would agree to the dispatch of U.S. troops to save a regime in North Africa. When the king was overthrown, if any idea of using force to restore him existed in Washington, it was overshadowed by concern over the practical problems of reversing a revolution in a large desert country and the safety of several thousand private U.S. citizens working in Libya.

Washington assumes that nations are eager to have the conspicuous presence of the United States represented by military forces or facilities. Despite the distance from World War II and the emergence of a strong sense of non-alignment in the Third World, many officials in U.S. administrations still assume that most nations want to be considered part of the "free world" and therefore want to be under U.S. protection. It comes as a surprise to many Americans when nations suggest that close military cooperation with the United States creates a political problem for them. In 1967, in a renegotiation of the Wheelus Base agreement, King Idris concurred in an extension of the U.S. rights only if the agreement accepted "the principle of withdrawal."

The fact is that few countries want the presence of foreign troops. So long as there is a consensus in the NATO countries on the Soviet threat, U.S. forces and facilities concentrating on that threat will be welcome. In the rest of the world, and particularly in the former colonies, the recollection of occupying troops and the legitimate concern over the cultural and social problems presented by foreign soldiers will hinder public support for the presence of foreign military facilities. If such countries decide to cooperate with the United States, it is because they hope the relationship will be beneficial to them.

The most common quid pro quo for base rights is some form of military assistance, either through grants of weapons and equipment or through sales. If the regime is dominated by the military, such U.S. assistance helps to keep the troops happy. A civilian regime in a friendly country involved in a regional conflict will seek help for its defense. Whatever the real motives for seeking U.S. assistance, the sophisticated leaders of a country will couch their requests in terms that sound valid to Washington—usually by stressing their resolute opposition to a communist menace. Such an approach, even if it may at times be challengeable, helps justify the request for assistance to the Congress.

The importance of the transfer of military equipment in the diplomacy of the United States means that embassies, including both diplomats and members of the military advisory groups attached to the embassy, become heavily involved in discussions of a foreign nation's military needs. Congress must review all sales of military equipment above a certain dollar limit, but the initiative on such sales rests with the executive branch. Policies of U.S. administrations have varied widely; those of the Carter administration sought to limit the transfer of arms, those of the Nixon administration gave virtual carte blanche to the shah of Iran to purchase the most sophisticated U.S. weapons. My one mission to the shah, in July 1978, was to dissuade him from purchasing F-18 aircraft.

Pressures for sophisticated weapons come not only from the military of the country, but also from the American manufacturers that seek to stimulate the desire of foreign countries for their products. The American diplomat seeking to limit sales has to contend with both groups. It is hard to avoid the impression at times, also, that some U.S. military advisers, with their eye on future employment, are on the side of the suppliers.

Despite major efforts to bolster strategic assets through military relationships, the United States has encountered setbacks in such key countries as Iraq, Iran, Ethiopia, and Libya. Many of these foreign policy setbacks were the result of efforts to apply the European experience to other areas of the world. NATO represented a model alliance; therefore, the pattern should be extended to other areas. Strong efforts were made in the 1950s to create NATO counterparts in the Middle East and East Asia through the Baghdad Pact and the South East Asia Treaty Organization (SEATO). They failed in large measure because the participants in the non-European areas had different objectives than the United States.

John Foster Dulles promoted the Baghdad Pact of Iraq, Iran, Turkey, and Pakistan as a "northern tier" bulwark against the Soviet Union. Pakistan's interest in military cooperation with the United States was related as much to its quarrel with India as to its concern over the Soviet Union. Iran had regional ambitions and pretensions. The Iraqis saw their cooperation in the pact as leverage on the Americans to wean the United States away from its solid support of Israel. Cooperation with the United States was not popular within Iraq.

I accompanied the U.S. chargé d'affaires in Baghdad when, after many delays, the Iraqi foreign minister signed a military assistance agreement with the United States but resigned immediately afterward. Washington noted the signing as an accomplishment. Some months later, I was back in Washington as the desk officer for Iraq in the Department of State. I was sent to meet Nuri al-Said, the prime minister of Iraq and strong man of that country, at Union Station in Washington and accompany him to the meeting with Secretary Dulles. In the most dramatic terms Prime Minister Nuri pleaded with Dulles to change U.S. policy toward the Pal-

estine question. Dulles turned away the pleas, emphasizing
the common interest of Iraq and the United States in con-
taining the Soviet menace in the area. Not long afterward,
Nuri's government was overthrown in a coup by strong anti-
Israel elements in the Iraq Army, and Nuri was torn apart in
the streets by a mob.

American diplomacy, particularly in strategic matters,
proceeds on the illusion that other nations share the U.S.
world perspective. People and regimes are placed in peril by
American policies because the United States, pursuing its
interests, ignores the political realities of other lands.

Difficulties in U.S. strategic relationships have been created not only by differences over objectives, but also by the
physical presence of U.S. forces. The U.S. military, with strong
congressional backing, insists that "status of forces" agreements be negotiated wherever troops are stationed that ex-
empt military personnel from local laws and jurisdictions.
Few aspects of the American presence are less popular but, in
many countries, more necessary to prevent trials and arrests
that would bring strong reactions in the United States. In
each of the countries with U.S. facilities in which I have
served the United States has faced continued pressure by the
government to narrow the range of exemptions. The foreign
governments, in such cases, were probably not wrong about
the possible political repercussions of the status of forces
problem. Among the many complaints that the Ayatollah
Khomeini had against the United States and the government
of the shah, none seemed to be stronger than that the shah
permitted U.S. servicemen to have a special status in Iran.

Americans often wonder why the United States is seen by
other countries as militant, if not bellicose. The heavy defense
expenditures of the USSR can be masked in a closed society.
This is not the case in the United States where discussions of
the defense budget, new weapons systems, the possibilities of
waging war, and military solutions to regional issues can be
observed by the whole world.

The interminable conferences that are part of American life often present international affairs largely in terms of a continuing conflict with the Soviet Union and its surrogates. These presentations are often simplistic, ignoring many of the complexities of recent history and of a multipolar world. On an assumption of ultimate conflict with the Soviets, the emphasis is less on how to avoid the conflict than it is on how to prepare for it. Such conferences are often supported by those who have a vested interest in major defense expenditures. Admittedly, serious issues are at stake and need to be examined, but such conferences on occasion present a warped picture to the American public and to the world both of the possibilities for U.S. military action and the American approach to diplomacy.

In spite of this attraction to the use of force, the United States does not have a strong record of success in the military support of diplomatic objectives. Time and again I have seen efforts to apply a military presence to a diplomatic circumstance fail, whether they involved sending carriers to the Bay of Bengal during an Indo-Pakistan war, attempts to rescue hostages in Iran, or retaliations against Lebanese tribesmen in the mountains above Beirut.

The effective use of U.S. forces to support foreign policy goals is handicapped by unrealistic expectations of what force will accomplish, by a lack of international support, and by the difficulty of maintaining the secrecy of operations.

The U.S. penchant is not just for military action but for quick military action. Force is seen as quick and decisive and preserves the American sense of honor and power. A successful deployment of force is popular no matter what the scale, whether it is the recovery of the *Mayaguez* or the bombing of Tripoli. Criticism of the use of force is usually not on the principle but on the failure to be successful.

Americans seem to believe that their nation has the capacity for the instantaneous deployment of large numbers of troops over great distances. In the demands to reverse an

Iranian revolution or protect regimes in the Persian Gulf, logistics are given little attention. At best, for example, at least two weeks would be required to place a credible force in the Gulf—by which time a revolution against a regime friendly to the United States would be consolidated. The task for the U.S. forces would then be to attack the new regime rather than to protect an old one. This view of the ease of action means that Americans are in constant danger of underestimating the obstacles to effective military action for limited objectives. As a result, as in the case of Vietnam, what starts as a limited action becomes a full-scale, unpopular major war. Some of the proposals that were made in discussions of the Iran crisis in 1978–79 seemed to be made without sufficient awareness of the vastness, aridity, and distance of Iran or of the international risks. A common suggestion during that crisis was for the United States to seize a southern Iranian province and establish a regime friendly to U.S. interests—which not only failed to take into account the Soviet right to intervene under the Iran-USSR agreement of 1921, but also ignored the dangers of the Soviet exploitation of a fragmented Iran.

Americans also possess a faith in the deterrence capacity of the presence of armed forces when applied to smaller nations. It is hard, from my experience, to document any situation in which the neighboring presence of U.S. forces has deterred a country from undertaking an unfriendly act. The risks to the United States in the deployment of forces to intimidate are two: that a foreign ruler will appeal to nationalist sensitivies and use the perceived foreign threat to rally his nation, and that he will use the threat as an excuse to seek aid from America's adversaries.

Despite this penchant, the public and the nature of American society put limits on the use of military force in support of diplomacy. Public doubts about long-term conflict and commitments have undoubtedly sparked congressional resistance to greater involvement in Nicaragua. Public support for the further deployment of U.S. troops far from American shores for more than a quick strike is unlikely.

Where U.S. forces have been used to support a diplomatic objective, the action has often been with little or no international support. The international community generally recognizes the right of a nation to use force to protect its citizens and to maintain armistices and peace agreements. The armed forces of the United States have been used for both purposes. Less international support exists for the use of outside forces to preserve a regime against internal revolution or to change a regime considered unfriendly by the intervening power. The use of armed force to retaliate for a terrorist act is likely to have even less international support, particularly if the retaliation seems out of proportion to the original act.

The lack of support by allies or their active criticism has been especially frustrating to the United States. Examples include the refusal to permit the use of European airfields in the U.S. troop movements to the Middle East in 1967 and 1973 and the French refusal of overflight rights to the United States in the bombing of Libya in 1986. Allies with strong trade and energy interests in the Middle East were not eager to antagonize Arab states. In general, the Europeans see regional issues differently from the United States and are not enthusiastic about military interventions. The one exception relates to France's commitments in Africa; even in these cases, France tends to be more cautious than the United States in such interventions. In early 1987, Chad forced the retreat of an invading Libyan army. French help was obviously crucial, but the French played down their role and gave primary credit to Chad. The United States had earlier expressed its impatience with France in Chad, but subsequently acknowledged the effectiveness of the French approach.

The use of military force by the United States in support of diplomacy has frequently been criticized abroad because of international skepticism regarding the precise American objectives. Although legitimate arguments exist for ambiguity in pursuing foreign policy goals, the advantages disappear when the ambiguity leads to confusion and an appearance of outright dissembling. The problem is particularly difficult for a major power; whatever the rationale that may be given for an action, the event is seen by much of the world in terms of the strategic ambitions of that power. In the case of the United States, rhetoric from Washington helps create this impression. When the United States sent the Marines to Lebanon in 1984 following the Israeli invasion, the inference was that they were there in a peacekeeping role. The explanatory rhetoric in Washington, however, put the invasion of Lebanon in an East-West context and spoke of the U.S. military presence as a further guarantee against Soviet gains in the region. The credibility of the U.S. peace-keeping role was further eroded by the shelling of the Druze villages and the open collaboration with Christian elements in Lebanon. The United States lost its credibility as a mediator. This action was significantly different from the U.S. deployment of military forces to Lebanon in 1958 when the military action was followed by active and successful American efforts to bring peace to the country.

Another rationale frequently given by the United States for the movement of military units or the use of force is the protection of U.S. citizens. This was used in the case of the Grenada intervention, although it was immediately clear from statements in Washington that the operation was more related to the Cuban presence on the island. The argument that U.S. citizens are being protected is often specious because the plans for the evacuation of U.S. citizens in emergencies generally call for the use of civilian aircraft and ships. Armed elements in a region of tension are not likely to distinguish between U.S. forces coming ashore to rescue citizens and those coming ashore to attack an unfriendly regime. In most cases, U.S. citizens have been evacuated with the acquiescence of the local government without the presence of U.S. armed forces.

Whatever the rationale for the action, the nature of U.S. society makes even the subtle deployment of our forces difficult. During the early days of the Iranian crisis, the United States planned to move helicopters and Marines near the border of Iran for a possible evacuation of U.S. citizens from that country. The Turks, extremely sensitive about any foreign troop deployments that are not directly linked to NATO, were prepared to accept the helicopters and Marines so long as the deployment was secret. Before the Marines even boarded their transports on the way to Turkey, word leaked out to the press from the staging base at Camp Lejeune, North Carolina. The Turks cancelled the permission.

In 1978, the National Democratic Front of southern Yemen, backed by the leftist government of the People's Democratic Republic of South Yemen, attacked the government of the northern republic. In coordination with Saudi Arabia, the United States sought to shore up the resistance of the government of the republic of Yemen in Sana. It was decided to send an aircraft carrier into the Indian Ocean from the U.S. Naval Base at Subic Bay in the Philippines. The hope was that, at some later time, the presence of the carrier presence in the area might be both psychologically and militarily helpful. In order not to inflame the situation at the moment, it was decided that the movement should be kept secret in its early stages. The story broke in the press within 24 hours of the decision to move the carrier. The report was not based on a high-level leak in Washington or anywhere else. A sailor off the carrier telephoned his mother in a small town in Nebraska before the ship left Subic Bay and said they were setting sail for the Indian Ocean. The telephone operator in the small town, also a stringer for the United Press, alerted the wire service to the action.

Whatever the circumstances, diplomats are generally unenthusiastic about the use of force, feeling that it is too often the preferred option and that diplomatic alternatives are given too little consideration. Two examples, as this is being written, illustrate the diplomats' dilemma: the U.S. intervention in Grenada in 1984 and the attack on Libya in 1986. In both cases, the military actions appear to have achieved their stated goals. In the case of Grenada, the American students were rescued and a democratic regime installed. The Libyan action seems to have ended the cycle of terrorist acts in which Qaddafi was involved. Neither the Grenada invasion nor the Libyan attack appear to have triggered regional reactions against the United States of the kind experienced after even less provocative actions in earlier years. The principal cost appears to have been in increasing the doubt of America's European allies about the steadfastness of U.S. policies. To this American diplomat, at least, both actions would have been more justified if the military option had not so clearly been the choice from the beginning of the Reagan administration. Having been the Secretary of State ad interim between the Carter and Reagan administrations, I was keenly aware that the elimination of the Cuban presence in Grenada and the Qaddafi regime in Libya were primary objectives of the new leadership. They were waiting for suitable opportunities; possible diplomatic moves to end the provocations were never given serious attention.

Diplomats do not question the close and necessary relationship between diplomacy and military action. When employed judiciously to deter actions against U.S. interests or to support a genuine peacekeeping effort, the military is a significant help to diplomacy. But when deployed in peripheral situations in which the support for the action either at home or in the field is not assured, the consequences can be tragic. Diplomacy must then be called on, without the military support, to solve the problems that existed before the action.

XIII

✐

DIPLOMACY AND
ECONOMIC ASSISTANCE

ECONOMIC ASSISTANCE is an obvious weapon in the contest for global influence, one particularly appropriate to American traditions and inclinations. Yet, in the United States, foreign economic assistance has become one of the most unpopular aspects of foreign policy and diplomacy. Much U.S. diplomatic effort today nevertheless relates to aid to developing countries: providing it, promoting it, denying it, negotiating it, observing it.

As one of my early bosses, a cynical old-school veteran of diplomatic wars, said to me when our economic aid programs were in their infancy: "Our foreign policy is becoming one of doing 'em good and making 'em like it." This was to become even more true as the years went on. And Americans asked increasingly, If we have done so much good, why are we not more appreciated?

The United States has been generous, and countries and peoples have been helped, but neither U.S. expectations nor those of the receiving countries have ever been fully met. At the heart of the matter is the sensitive relationship between donor and recipient. Proud nations and their leaders are uncomfortable receiving aid. They like even less the intrusions of foreign control and advice that accompany such aid.

In the United States, resources for foreign assistance must compete with domestic demands. The resulting need of an administration to demonstrate to the public and to the Congress that such assistance is in the U.S. national interest rubs the raw nerves of nations receiving the support.

Symbolic of the unpopularity of foreign assistance is the fact that its legislative life for many years depended on the leadership support of one of its sharpest critics—a congressman from Louisiana, Otto Passman. Although vocal in his criticism, Passman successfully steered foreign aid legislation through the House of Representatives for many years. He cloaked his success in often startling rhetorical attacks against the whole concept. I was a witness before him on one occasion when he opened the hearing thus: "Foreign aid is the worst disaster this nation has suffered since the War of 1812. But, of course, Mr. Newsom, I can't expect you to agree with that because you have your feet in the public trough."He then turned to the stenographer and said, "Strike that from the record," and an intense grilling over individual projects and their fate followed.

A recent Congressional Research Service (CRS) paper describes what has happened to U.S. attitudes toward foreign assistance:

> Americans—and Congress especially—quickly became disillusioned with foreign aid. This disillusionment spread and deepened over two decades, reaching its peak with the fall of Vietnam, where massive infusions of military aid, development assistance, and budget support were unable to promote stable and effective government or sustained economic growth, let alone provide a successful antidote to communist subversion and expansion. Why this sense of false expectation and subsequent disillusionment?
>
> Primarily because we expected foreign aid to work in Asia, and subsequently in Latin America and the Middle East, much as it had worked in Western Europe. Just as Western Europe had

been thrown off course by World War II, Asia had been thrown off course by colonialism. With infusions of money, military support, and technical assistance, many Americans expected to have new nations of Asia on their feet in a few more years than it had taken for the nations of Europe, able to withstand communism on their own.

The United States, as a nation, is still coming to terms with just how wrong those expectations were. We are still learning just how much is involved in building the institutions, the leadership, the knowledge, and the personal beliefs that are necessary to sustain economic growth alongside even moderate levels of political freedom.

Many Americans were shocked to discover that the governments, as well as the economies, of the countries we were trying to help were undeveloped: they were often inept, corrupt, and repressive. Many were angered when our military aid was used to repress legitimate opponents of the regimes we supported. Many were outraged when our military and economic aid lined the pockets of the already well-to-do. Many were frustrated when even the well-meaning recipients of our aid were unable to use our money and advice to promote growth.*

Genuine sympathy for foreign assistance exists among only a few. The more general comment is: "It's our money, isn't it? Why shouldn't we do what we like with it? If they don't like our conditions, they know what they can do." Domestic concerns have priority; I have been asked to explain to a congressional committee why I think a road in Zaire is more important to the United States than a road in Nebraska.

Americans believe that the United States, in comparison with other industrialized countries, is doing more than its share; other nations should do more and on more generous terms. Americans are shocked to learn that their country ranks thirteen in per capita economic assistance to developing countries, but these attitudes do not change. The belief in our generosity is sustained by the fact that in overall

*Stanley J. Heginbotham, *An Overview of U.S. Foreign Aid Programs* (Congressional Research Service, April 19, 1985).

dollar terms we still provide the largest amount in foreign aid of any nation.

The feeling abroad exists, nevertheless, that it is the United States that is not doing its share. The wealth and strength Americans display through life styles, movies, television, and the sheer statistics of the U.S. economy have led many foreign leaders to expect that aid would be provided out of a sense of duty and that the capacity existed to provide what was needed. The fact that, in the perception of many countries, the United States did not meet these expectations led to diminished U.S. influence in many Third World countries.

To this perception was added the belief that the United States was basically uninterested in, if not unsympathetic to, helping the poorer countries—a belief created by the constant U.S. opposition to international proposals to set goals for the transfer of resources to the developing countries. These proposals have included that of Canadian Prime Minister Lester Pearson in 1969 that the developed nations commit .07 percent of gross national product to development, the report on development objectives of German Chancellor Willy Brandt in 1980, and the New International Economic Order. The United States, as the world's largest potential donor, has admittedly been the primary target of international pressures for specific dollar commitments to development. Although most of the proposals have been symbolic and, for the United States, impractical, the American rejection has been exploited by others as an indication of our lack of interest in the developing world.

U.S. support for international economic assistance programs has also been affected by the tendency of Third World nations to introduce what Americans see as extraneous political issues into conferences on foreign aid. The most common example is the introduction by Arab governments of Palestinian-related issues into United Nations committees on economic development. Washington has compounded the problem by introducing what others see as political issues into the proceedings of the international lending agencies. Under congressional pressure, for example, the United States has sought to restrict World Bank lending to Vietnam and to the Nicaraguan government. Although it helped create these agencies and an American has always headed the World Bank, the United States was never able to exert the degree of control Congress desired, and the relationship between the U.S. government, U.S. diplomats, and bank representatives, both in Washington and abroad, has always been tenuous.

What is true in other U.S. foreign policy programs is true in aid: the most popular activities are those that bring dramatic results in a short space of time. The United States responds enthusiastically to immediate and dramatic human needs: starvation in Biafra, a famine in Ethiopia, an earthquake in Turkey. That enthusiasm does not extend to long-range development of the type that would serve, over time, to correct conditions that bring on disasters. Early efforts to gain multi-year commitments of aid from the Congress were successful, but the general disillusionment over performance versus expectations and the erosion of legislative control has meant that Congress will now only appropriate on a carefully monitored year-by-year basis.

Modern peacetime foreign aid began with massive assistance to the countries of Western Europe through the Marshall Plan following World War II. In the years between 1947 and 1953, the annual level of that aid was greater than the total amount of our subsequent aid to developing countries in all but two peak years. A primary aim of the Marshall Plan was to rebuild Europe in order to prevent the spread of communism. As the sense of need shifted to less developed areas of the world, the anticommunist motive remained, but others arose. Early assistance was based on the concept that poverty and hopelessness bred communism; the political and humanitarian motives were linked.

Americans discovered that economic development in the

newer countries was more difficult to achieve than it had been in a Europe which, although ravaged by war, had the institutional, educational, and cultural infrastructure for recovery and growth.

In the tortured history of efforts to reconcile the diverse American domestic views toward foreign aid with the needs and attitudes of recipient nations, the U.S. diplomat works against a backdrop of disillusionment in the United States, conflicting objectives in the Congress, and competing political priorities in the executive. Few items rank lower on the scale of popularity in Congress than foreign aid legislation, yet few of the tools of U.S. diplomacy are more important.

The newness of the issue of assistance to the less developed countries led to sharp debates in the United States over the objectives and philosophies of economic assistance. Mutual security, political influence, humanitarian objectives, trade benefits, private investment, and basic human needs have vied over the life of the aid program for priority attention in the allocation of funds. Advocates of multilateral aid argued that a greater proportion should be channeled through the international organizations. In those relatively rare years when foreign aid bills have been passed, passage has been possible only through assembling a successful coalition of supporters of each of these motives. Levels and approaches to aid fluctuated as one philosophy or another became dominant.

Although the emphasis has varied from administration to administration, the United States, in its assistance philosophy, has always sought to promote the indigenous private sector. In many countries this is a sensitive issue. The private sector is often in the hands of minorities not favored by the rulers. Those enterprises favored by the ruler may be ones in which the ruling family has a financial interest. Efforts to provide contracts to established private firms may be looked on with suspicion: Is the United States seeking to give political power to this or that group?

Philosophically, the emphasis stems from a basic American attitude against government enterprise, at home or abroad. It is another facet of the belief that the newly independent countries should resemble the early American example with the private sector in the forefront of development.

In addition to the questions of minority dominance and conflicts of interest, other problems accompany this emphasis on the private sector. Multinational corporations can play an important role, but their objective is profit, not development. Local investors want a quick return on investment; the long-term climate is too uncertain. Sources of credit and capital are undeveloped. Retail trade is preferred over industry.

As the global confrontation with the Soviets heightened in the 1950s, the strategic aspect of foreign aid became paramount. Nations became important because of their location and their willingness to join in regional defense pacts. Their importance was reflected in levels of assistance based more on that factor than on the capacity of the nation to develop.

The question of competing motives for foreign aid became symbolized in debates over assistance to individual countries. India was popular with those who wanted development for development's sake. Pakistan was popular with those who wanted a strategic emphasis, the Ivory Coast and Singapore with the advocates of the private sector. Israel and Egypt and those countries with U.S. military facilities, however, subsequently came to receive the lion's share of U.S. economic aid.

The shifting priorities of aid were accompanied by constant reorganizations and agency name changes. The "pure developers" wanted a review pattern that would exclude political considerations, in which proponents of economic aid would report directly to the president and aid would be dispensed without "strings." Secretaries of state have avoided assuming operational responsibility, but have been successful in maintaining a review authority to permit consideration of political and diplomatic factors. Beginning as the Mutual

Security Administration (MSA), the agency has been known at various times as the Foreign Operations Administration (FOA), the International Cooperation Administration (ICA—unfortunately confused with CIA when translated into other languages), and finally the Agency for International Development (AID).

Against this welter of domestic limitations and foreign expectations, the U.S. diplomat must conceive, explain, negotiate, and monitor foreign assistance programs. This involves, in nearly every level of activity, fitting the concepts and priorities of the United States together with the needs and political realities of another society. Nowhere is this more apparent than in negotiations that take place on aid programs.

The mission director of the Agency for International Development and that unit's staff will undertake the basic negotiations on a country program. The mission director will work under the burden of a volume of instructions—do's and dont's from Washington. Each year, the worldwide U.S. emphasis may be different. In one, the stress may be on community development; in another it may be on pilot projects in agriculture. The foreign recipient must be persuaded to respond to such priorities.

The receiving country, however, may have in mind a different set of needs: roads, bridges, schools. Patiently, the AID negotiators must suggest other donors for the major capital projects and stress the wisdom and uniqueness of what the United States can provide.

In recent years, to save the assistance program, the emphasis in the choice of projects has been on "basic human needs." Major capital projects were to be the responsibility of the international lending agencies. Such a policy, its proponents believed, would reduce the degree to which the United States was identified with grandiose projects or corrupt gains of authoritarian rulers. The U.S. aid would get to the people. The policy, however, had some ironic twists. One interpretation decreed that this meant that U.S. technicians should work directly at the grass roots or village level. Where previously a U.S. expert earning $50,000 per year might have been teaching nationals of a country at an institutional center, that expert was assigned to a village.

Support for the development of national institutions, such as universities or research institutes, was rejected as being too open ended and as catering to an elite. This policy change failed totally to appreciate the advantages of multiplying the influence of highly paid U.S. technicians through work at the national level. It meant also that under a strict interpretation of this policy the United States could no longer fund higher education for foreign university graduates. The previous policy had created an impressive number of men and women who later carried the burden of development in their own countries. I was one of many U.S. ambassadors who pointed out the shortsightedness of such a policy. It was later modified.

Negotiations at times involved the question of who would get the credit for assistance projects, whose name would appear on the billboards. The United States vacillated on this question. One year every effort would be made to insure that the United States received the credit—in large letters. In another year the emphasis was on the host country.

Here again the policy of "basic human needs" created ironies. Designed to reduce the degree of U.S. identification with a ruling elite, in some countries it had the opposite effect. An authoritarian ruler often appeals largely to a rural population. The urban intellectuals, in the ruler's mind, represent a threat. In the Philippines, for example, an aid program that reduced the number of grants to those at the university level and emphasized village projects played into the hands of the Marcos regime. I attended the opening of a village project paid for by the United States and stood with some embarrassment under a sign that suggested the project had come through the leadership and generosity of Ferdinand and Imelda Marcos.

Negotiations on assistance projects are also extremely technical. They range over issues of the sale of commodities, the rates of exchange, the reporting requirements, as well as questions of customs privileges and the status of U.S. technicians.

Foreign leaders who are sensitive to U.S. realities craft appeals for aid on the basis of their professed anticommunism, needs, and expressed willingness to cooperate with the United States in unspecified ways. Leaders in developing countries have at times felt an almost desperate need to obtain substantial U.S. aid not only because of actual need, but because of political and economic promises made to their populations.

The U.S. diplomat must answer by trying to explain an extraordinarily complicated legislative process that has, over the years, produced a variety of forms of aid; Congressman Passman used to call them spigots. The diplomat abroad must help a foreign official unfamiliar with U.S. procedures to sort out the difference between Development Assistance, Technical Assistance, Supporting Assistance, Public Law 480 and its various Titles, and Commodity programs.* That done, the diplomat must then try to explain how levels of aid are decided.

An embassy and the AID mission that administers the program may reach agreement with a government on what the needs are and on the level of assistance necessary to meet those needs—as seen from the viewpoint of the country. That

---

*Development Assistance: grants or loans for specific development projects. Technical Assistance: grants or loans to support technicians for training and demonstration projects. Supporting Assistance: grants or loans usually designed to assist countries economically that are receiving military assistance. Public Law 480: the grants, credits, or sales to support the provision of U.S. agricultural commodities. Various titles of the act specify help for emergency relief, food-for-work and long-range development. Commodity programs: Credits to enable a country to purchase commodities from the U.S. for resale for local currency.

recommendation then goes to Washington. The proposal is trimmed to fit an overall appropriations request to the Congress. Bureaucrats in the annual process of "cutting the pie" fight for the highest possible allocation of aid funds for their region. Inevitably, in this process every region becomes of "vital importance." The policymaker must sort out the reality from dozens of frequently exaggerated rhetorical rationalizations for high aid levels. Congress may cut that further. The end result may be less money and different priorities from those originally agreed on at the country level with the foreign government.

The disappointment in a capital can be severe, for to most foreign politicians the published level of aid is the most important item of all. This demonstrates graphically their ability to "get something" for their country. The actual projects may be less important; those are left to the technicians.

Not all leaders are as direct as the Imam of Yemen in 1957. Following the passage of the joint congressional resolution on the Middle East—the Eisenhower Doctrine—former Congressman James P. Richards set out on a regional journey to dispense $200 million in special emergency assistance to those countries that would endorse the doctrine. When Richards reached Yemen, he announced to the Imam that if Yemen supported the U.S. view toward the Middle East, the United States was prepared to provide $2 million in economic assistance funds. The Imam asked Richards how many countries he was visiting. "Fourteen," said Richards. The Imam remarked that $200 million divided by 14 was not $2 million and he expected his fair share. On being told this was not possible, the Iman walked out and the interview was over.

Aid levels become a matter of national pride. For a number of years, because of the importance of the Middle East peace process, Israel and Egypt have taken the bulk of U.S. economic assistance. Other countries friendly to the United States have complained that they had a "lower priority" and have insisted that they should have as much. U.S. diplomats have been required to explain and defend these allocations, often to unsympathetic listeners.

The problem is compounded because aid levels are public and the process by which they are established is public. Amounts often emerge from Congress before they are discussed with foreign governments. After the Soviet invasion of Afghanistan, Pakistan became especially vulnerable. The Carter administration decided that increased aid to Pakistan was justified and began discussions with the Congress. They were not easy because General Zia al-Huq and his rule were not popular with many in the Congress. A figure of $200 million leaked out of the congressional deliberations. Before any U.S. diplomat had had the opportunity to discuss it with President Zia, a newspaper reporter asked Zia whether this amount would be satisfactory. In a well-publicized reply, he termed it "peanuts." He was comparing it with what the United States was planning to do in the same fiscal year for Israel and Egypt.

The Soviet Union and some other donors treat the question of levels differently. They will frequently announce a line of credit of a fairly substantial amount. The receiving country is then able to announce impressive "help" from the Soviet Union before negotiations have taken place over individual projects. The U.S. Congress has always insisted that agreement on projects and costs come first.

As the years have gone by, both the Congress and administrations have added specific requirements and restrictions to the aid legislation; "barnacles," they are called. For example, well-meaning members of Congress have said, "I think we should pay attention to the role of women in development." That simple suggestion becomes a line in the legislation and a requirement for a report relating this factor to each new aid project. When similar considerations of population policy, narcotics policy, economic policies, and environmental concerns are added, a justification for a single aid project may run well over a hundred pages. Lawyers in the agency put the strictest possible interpretation on it, having been "shell-shocked" over the years by accusations that they have not followed congressional mandates. A Moroccan finance minister said to me some years ago when I was negotiating an assistance package with him and outlined these requirements, "To do all you want I need three Harvard Ph.D.s on my staff and I have only one in the country."

Then there is the matter of the number of Americans necessary to administer an aid program. When I was in Jakarta, the Australians administered with six people an aid program at a level roughly the same as ours. We had over eighty with their dependents and all the inevitable problems of a conspicuous, affluent presence in a relatively poor country. Efforts by ambassadors to hold down the numbers are invariably unsuccessful given the pressures of the "needs."

The answer again comes back to the system. The need to inform Congress of each detail of the implementation of an aid program means that we cannot leave the implementation, as many other countries do, largely to the local officials. U.S. missions also contain many experts who provide a necessary and important contribution to the programs. Other countries depend less on technical experts and more on a direct transfer of funds to the country.

When other issues have been resolved in the negotiations, the issue of the quid pro quo remains. This question of what the country will provide in exchange for the aid may need to be reconciled by a discussion between a high official of the receiving government and the U.S. ambassador—or perhaps a special emissary from Washington.

Both sides in an assistance negotiation like to give the impression that they are motivated solely by the needs of the people of a developing country. Both sides also know that this is not so. There is another agenda. The United States does not provide large amounts of aid without receiving something in return. It may be support for a policy, a military facility, a Voice of America transmitter, or an effort to preempt a Soviet initiative. The officials of the receiving country have their objectives as well. They want to demonstrate that their leadership can produce substantial gains, without violating their independence or sovereignty. Sometimes the relationship between the aid and the quid is never even mentioned; it is only understood.

In 1963, I accompanied Averell Harriman, then under secretary of state, on a trip to Ethiopia. The trip was stimulated by intelligence that the emperor was considering recognizing the People's Republic of China. The United States still maintained its policy of discouraging friendly countries from such an act. The emperor was in need of additional assistance. The figure of $8 million had been mentioned in lower-level discussions.

Harriman and the emperor were one month apart in age. Each was a wily veteran of his political system. They met in the emperor's office. Haile Selassie sat at an ornate desk at one end of the room. Two rows of chairs, facing each other, had been arranged at right angles to his desk. Ethiopian ministers sat on one side facing Harriman, the U.S. ambassador, and me on the other.

The conversation lasted for three hours, followed by lunch. Each time the emperor appeared to be approaching the subject of aid, Harriman would interrupt with some recollection of his trip to Asmara in 1945. Each time Harriman seemed to be nearing a political subject, the emperor would change the conversation. The emperor's ministers, impatient, began sending notes to him.

At the end of the day, I was to draft the telegram, a first-person telegram from Harriman to the secretary of state. Since I could not recall that either aid or China had been mentioned, I wrote a final paragraph: "While I believe we have an understanding with the emperor, I noted on a shelf in his office as we left that the elaborate ivory statue donated by the People's Republic of China was still in place."

Harriman called me in. "Why did you write that?" "I believe we succeeded," I said, "but I am not absolutely sure." "When I go on a mission," said Harriman, "it succeeds." He took a pencil and struck out the offending phrase. As it turned out, he was right; it was several years before the Ethiopians recognized the People's Republic of China.

A number of questions relating to economic assistance can never be fully answered. Does our assistance improve the lives of people? Does it support elites and governments? Does it give us influence we would not otherwise have? How important are the levels of aid over the fact that we give it? The answers are complex. Economic development may not have the highest priority, even in poor countries. Weak or oppressive regimes are often reluctant to take the risks required for genuine development. Corruption or self-aggrandizement may divert resources badly needed for economic purposes. Foreign assistance is often not popular among the population of a country, particularly the educated portion. However it is described, U.S. help is seen by opponents of a regime in authoritarian countries as support for the government in power.

One of the most difficult questions to answer is how much political influence Washington gains through economic assistance programs. Congress clearly anticipates that the provision of aid can provide leverage to achieve U.S. political and economic objectives. The provision of aid, as previously pointed out, has been tied to human rights considerations. Legislation prohibits aid to communist countries; efforts have been made to extend this to the lending by multilateral institutions. Two pieces of legislation, the Hickenlooper and Gonzalez amendments, are intended to protect U.S. companies against nationalization through cutting off an aid program. The Glenn amendment requires the termination of aid in countries with non-safeguarded nuclear projects. The

Brook amendment makes it necessary to terminate aid when a nation is in arrears on its debts to the United States.*

These are all logical expressions of a donor country's interests. The problem is that they seldom achieve their objectives. As in the implementation of the human rights legislation, the threat is more powerful than the application. I am not aware of cases in which the application of either Hickenlooper or Gonzalez has restored nationalized U.S. properties; the attempts to apply the legislation have created problems with Sri Lanka, Ethiopia, and Algeria. The U.S. interest in helping Pakistan on strategic grounds outweighed the force of the Glenn amendment in seeking to deter Pakistan's nuclear program.

My view is that the United States gains influence through an aid program by the long-term consistency of that program rather than through efforts to manipulate it for short-term gains. The cumbersome procedures of the aid program mean that the only real leverage is through terminating aid; this seldom appears to achieve the objective for which it was intended. It has been virtually impossible to fine tune the program so that countries can be rewarded for positive steps.

France has maintained its position in Africa in part because it maintains its aid to the francophone countries, despite changes of government, changes of policy, and short-term problems for France. The fact that the aid is consistent means that countries will be more inclined to consider France's basic interests over the long term.

U.S. ambassadors in developing countries generally believe some response to local development needs is essential if there is to be influence and access. Without aid, there may be little interest in other aspects of the U.S. presence. When, in the early 1970s, the number of countries in Africa receiving

---

*For principal limitations on U.S. economic assistance, see U.S. Code (1982 edition) Title 22, Section 2370. For the Glenn amendment see Title 22, Section 2429(a).

U.S. assistance was reduced, one ambassador told me, "My phone has stopped ringing."

Americans tend to exaggerate the degree of influence that can be gained through economic assistance—even over economic policies in a country. In very few countries does the United States provide the bulk of assistance. In some major countries, the U.S. proportion is small in relation to the countries of Europe or Japan. If the United States provides aid, it is because Washington believes such aid is needed; Americans should have no illusions regarding any substantial influence on local policies. An exception is when the United States is part of an international consortium, such as the Intergovernmental Group on Indonesia. In this highly successful arrangement, the donor countries meet with Indonesian officials and the World Bank and coordinate levels of assistance and economic policies.

The obstacles to effective economic assistance are many. But that day does come when the results—and the human aspects—can be seen. The results of an assistance program can often be intangible. One of them is motivation, the inspiration that comes from association with a particularly effective technician or from a demonstration that something indeed can be done. In my time as Assistant Secretary for Africa, this question of motivation came up again and again. Development is a state of mind. If it does not exist, projects may not create it. I once spent three days with the radical and unpredictable president of Guinea, Sékou Touré. His conversation was a monologue on African culture, governing, imperialism, colonialism, and socialism. He said to me at one point, "My greatest problem is motivating a population that can live off the land without any real work. I am afraid socialism does not have the answer." He continued, nevertheless, for many years to pursue a harsh socialist policy—with disastrous results for Guinea.

On another occasion I visited a prerevolutionary prime minister in Libya. As I entered, he said to me, obviously referring to the bedouin spirit of the country, "What do you do to get a country moving where it is considered honorable to sit for eight hours and do nothing?"

Although not officially part of our assistance programs, the Peace Corps has done wonders around the world in showing people that, with the right kind of effort, things can be done. Some years ago, I was at the opening of a six-kilometer road from a village in a West African country to a main road. Before the road was built, all the products of the village had to be portaged over a narrow path fording two streams. The road was made possible because an American technician, in this case a 61-year-old former telephone lineman from Chicago, had discovered a field of castaway truck chassis and had shown how, by welding the chassis together, small bridges could be built. His was the ingenuity and the motivation. The work was that of the villagers.

The opening was typical of such occasions: tables of fruit and sweets and unidentified soft drinks spread beneath a thatched canopy, speeches by local dignitaries dressed in their finest, children and mothers peering from behind trees, and a few words from the U.S. ambassador. After the ceremonies, I asked one of the villagers why, during all the years the village had been in existence, no one had ever before built an outlet road. His answer was simple, "No one ever told us we could do it."

I have, in the course of my career, had many such occasions: electricity turned on for the first time in a rural electrification project, a new water well in a village, a new dam on a great river, observing the work of those who have brought back the fruits of an American education. In each case, I have felt a sense of pride. I do not know if the results will be lasting, if the lights will still be on or the water flowing ten years from now. But on those special occasions, I felt that the labored turnings of our system, through whatever mixture of motivations, had produced, in the satisfaction of some distant villager and his identification of the work with my country, a laudable result.

XIV

✐

TELLING AMERICA'S STORY

A NAIVE BELIEF exists among Americans that if their policies
are not acceptable to others it is because the nation has not
been sufficiently effective in "selling" the policies.

In 1948, a new dimension was added to traditional U.S.
diplomacy to do just that. Impressed by the power of propaganda before and during World War II and compelled by the
evidence of Soviet information efforts, Congress and the administration created the United States Information Agency
(USIA) and its field counterpart, the United States Information Service (USIS). The Voice of America was established to
carry the radio message behind the Iron Curtain and around
the world. Press activities were organized. A wireless file
began to carry official statements and commentaries daily to
U.S. embassies. Library and film branches were designed to
tell others about the United States, its ideals, its culture, and
its objectives. Educational exchange, a stepchild, was placed
in the Department of State in Washington and in USIS offices
abroad; its purpose was to provide the framework for non-
political academic and cultural programs.

Other Western nations also organized overseas information and cultural activities to tell the world about themselves,

179

but the U.S. program was more ideological, designed to promote democracy and freedom in competition with the propaganda of the Soviet Union.

The concept was simple. Official programs, augmented by media talents and non-official institutions, would meet the challenge of its adversaries, make friends, and advance foreign policies of the United States. The organizers of USIA concluded that traditional diplomacy would not accomplish these objectives in a period when rapid communication and public attitudes seemed increasingly important in national decisions. Embassies were seen as restricted to government contacts and as distant from "the people." Private news agencies could not reach behind the Iron Curtain. If the United States government could have its own voice, so the argument went, the message would be clearer than the sometimes negative reporting of the private sector. A deep conviction existed that if the United States could get its story accurately to the peoples of the world, the truth and correctness of its vision of events would prevail.

Not every American shared this view. Traditional diplomats, at least at the beginning, treated the new agency with skepticism, if not outright opposition. If U.S. policy was to be explained, they believed it should be done through the foreign ministries and not by direct pleading with local journalists or opposition politicians. They were not enthusiastic about the new USIS officers who brought a concept of public relations alien to the more cautious and discreet practices of diplomacy. Many of the old-style ambassadors saw the only value of the new agency to be its ability to provide occasional films and cultural events for embassy functions.

Domestically, the private media opposed the concept. Was it really necessary to have an official information agency? Would not our own private channels effectively tell America's story? Was it not just a brief step from that agency to one that sought to mold domestic opinion in the United States? Opponents were able to obtain legislation that prohibited USIS from disseminating any material within the United States and established policies that severely restricted the news that could be distributed abroad in the USIS wireless file. Many of the original sources of opposition to this government information role have remained skeptics and watchdogs throughout the life of the agency.

In theory, some of the skepticism was justified. In practice, it has been extremely difficult to carry on effectively a government information program in the environment of free American democracy. USIA has fallen far short of its basic goal of creating broad international support for U.S. interests and policies. The organizers were naive in many respects. They imagined the international public environment to be fundamentally sympathetic to the American message. Instead, USIA's message has, like official policies, encountered a complex and occasionally hostile reception, even in areas outside Soviet influence.

Americans imagine themselves as free, democratic, innovative, generous, and peace-loving. They assume others see them that way. They are shocked that there are those outside the Soviet orbit who see them as neo-colonialists, aggressive, insensitive, ungenerous, and trigger-happy. They are angered that, while they see themselves as the standard-bearer of a "Free World," many in the world profess to see little to choose between the external policies of the United States and the Soviet Union. Over the years Americans have learned that most nations do not want to "stand up and be counted" in the contest between the superpowers, that nations are not inclined to acknowledge an outside threat from the Soviets unless it is near and real, that others regard both powers as aggressive, and that the international credibility of the United States is not as high as Americans imagine it to be.

I experienced the problem of "telling America's story" at first hand. During my career, I was twice assigned to the USIA, once to establish the program in the new state of Pakistan and once as public affairs officer in charge of the program in Iraq. Recognizing that the fundamental objective of the USIA was to create public support abroad for policies favorable to the United States, I had to ask myself on many occasions whether what I was doing was achieving that aim. As I gave a book to a schoolteacher or showed a film in a village, I often wondered, "What does this really accomplish?" The book and the film may have been appreciated, but how was one to know the true reaction of the recipient?

On one occasion the difference in simple perceptions came dramatically home. In Iraq I asked our projectionist to get reactions from the villagers when he showed films in a village. One popular film was a short Walt Disney documentary on malaria. It opened with a full screen view of a mosquito. When the projectionist asked one villager what he thought of the film, the villager replied, "It is a fine film, but it doesn't apply to us."

"Why?" asked the projectionist.

"Because our mosquitos are not that big."

On other occasions, I presented cultural events or made English language lessons available. I sent students to America, a portion of whom returned to useful livelihoods in their own country. Through lecturers from American universities I came to know intellectuals. I helped the ambassador by rushing texts of statements by the U.S. government to Foreign Ministry officials. But, even in friendly countries, the response to our policies and our political message was often lukewarm. On many occasions, I have been asked by fellow Americans, "With all the effort we are making, why are we not better understood and accepted for what we are? Why do we seem so often to be under attack? Why aren't we getting our story across?"

USIA has failed to do what many Americans expected, in part, because it was given a virtually impossible goal: to reconcile how Americans want others to see them with a more accurate view of what Americans are in reality. The world, in general, was not prepared to view the United States on its own terms or automatically to perceive it in a more favorable light than the Soviet Union.

At the time of the formation of USIA, there was wide agreement that the primary emphasis should be on countering Soviet efforts to discredit the United States and its policies. If there had not been a substantial Soviet effort to advance Marxism-Leninism and to strike at the interests of the United States, it is unlikely that the administration at the time and the Congress would ever have taken the precedent-breaking step of establishing an official information service in a time of peace.

From its inception, USIA was expected to promote U.S. policies without having a role, as an agency, in the formulation of the policies. As the difficulties of "selling" many of America's policies became apparent, some saw the solution in a closer coordination of "public diplomacy" and official diplomacy. The director of USIA sought a place at the table in national security policy making. As of this writing, nearly forty years after the establishment of the program, how policies will be perceived remains a minor factor in their creation. Currently in the Reagan administration, USIA director Charles Wick, as a close associate of the president, has a seat at the table. Considerable attention is given to the importance of public diplomacy. Policymakers seem to conclude, as they always have, that the proper techniques can sell any policy; if a policy fails it is less due to the policy than to how it is portrayed.

Arguments over the objectives of USIA have therefore not centered on whether the policy was correct, but on methods and approach. One school of thought in the agency and in the Congress has favored a positive presentation that emphasizes the United States, its values, life, and democratic institutions. Proponents of this approach believe that USIA material should give a "full and fair" picture of the United States, that the official information effort will only gain credibility if it shows negative as well as positive aspects of U.S. society and policies.

A second prefers an emphasis on aggressive broadsides against the Soviet Union and an exposure of the faults and failures of international communism, minimizing references to problems in U.S. society in the belief that such material will merely give ammunition to adversaries. Advocates of this have at times recommended tactics that are mirror images of what the Soviets do abroad: clandestine radios, subsidized newspapers, covert funding to journalists, the formation of front organizations. As the fate of the numerous clandestine operations of the 1950s has shown, the U.S. public will not knowingly support such covert activities. The CIA support of Radio Liberty, Radio Free Europe, several organizations, and journalists was ended by Congress in the 1970s.

The question of objectives arises in the management of each of the separate activities of USIA. Limitations of budget and resources dictate that choices must be made. The most conspicuous debate has been over the policies of the Voice of America, beginning with that of news coverage. Professional journalists employed by VOA, backed in recent years by strong support in the Senate, want complete freedom in the selection of news items. An ideological management may prefer to screen out that which may be contrary to policy or show the United States in a bad light. The degree of freedom seems to vary with circumstances and administrations.

The Voice has, over the years, broadcast much that is factual and objective. The VOA coverage of Watergate, for example, was remarkably full. As a listener over many years, however, I have an overall impression of bland news, tilting toward emphasizing the wrongs of our adversaries, strong anticommunist commentaries, and nonpolitical half-hour segments devoted to advances in agriculture, space, education, and art. The foreign language broadcasts of the VOA carry foreign music and cultural presentations with little political content that are designed to build listenership. And half-hours of rock or country music are broadcast to reach the newer generations.

In 1984 in Indonesia, I had the opportunity to listen to the Voice for the first time in six years. I found less attention to domestic U.S. events than before and an increased emphasis on items relating to regional conflicts and the activities of the Soviet Union and its surrogates. Coverage of congressional events seemed to report only that which was favorable to the administration; I did not hear the other side on such issues as aid to El Salvador or arms control policies.

On the evening before "Super Tuesday," March 13, 1984, when there were nine primaries and caucuses in the United States, there was no reference to these in the regular VOA news broadcasts. Instead, the ten-minute segment dealt with Lebanon, the Soviet Union, Germany, Sri Lanka, and Japan.

In such cases I and many other listeners have had to turn to the British Broadcasting Corporation's world service to learn what is happening in the United States. The Voice of America loses credibility in competition with a service which, whether accurately or not, is regarded as uninfluenced by British government policy. Without similar credibility, the Voice cannot hope to be effective in persuasively presenting elements of American foreign policy.

Clearly, one of VOA's primary and agreed objectives is the penetration of the Soviet Union and Eastern Europe. Here there is ample evidence of effectiveness. VOA brings news of actions not available from local sources. Some of the outlandish attacks made by Soviet media on the United States are corrected. This emphasis does not need to be incompatible with credibility as an independent source of news; in practice, however, it threatens VOA's standing in the rest of the world.

The existence of the Voice of America highlights another problem in American diplomacy, the compatibility of this public voice with our diplomatic efforts. Seldom do American ambassadors abroad know—until they listen—what the Voice of America may say about issues important at their post. Frequently they are called upon to explain or account for items on VOA considered critical of the foreign country or contrary to official U.S. policy. At times a diplomatic effort is clearly undercut.

At the close of the Nigerian civil war in 1970, when I was assistant secretary for African affairs, I was in Lagos. My instructions were to see General Yakabu Gowon, the Nigerian head of state, and seek to persuade him to accept an international commission to survey the reconstruction of Biafra, the secessionist area. This was a sensitive matter with the victorious Federal Military Government; any public mention of the U.S. interest was likely to kill it.

My appointment with General Gowon was at nine in the morning. As I was breakfasting at the American Embassy at seven, I listened to the Voice of America telling its listeners around the world—including Nigeria—that the U.S. assistant secretary of state for African affairs would see the Nigerian head of state that morning and urge him to accept an international commission in Biafra. Had there been any chance of successful diplomacy it died at that moment. That item, and undoubtedly others like it, were broadcast to satisfy an American domestic or congressional interest in the subject. Obviously little attention was given to its impact on U.S. diplomatic efforts.

Any Western international broadcasting service encounters the fact that the concept of an objective government radio service is alien to listeners in many countries. Officials in most Third World countries assume that what is broadcast, whether favorable or unfavorable, has been approved by the government. When the information appears to be in opposition to the government's interest, they look for some hidden motive. The Voice of America has less credibility than the BBC, and accordingly suffers more from this problem.

Television is adding a new dimension to the USIA pro-

gram. Where permitted by foreign countries, satellite trans-
missions bring presidential messages and U.S. information
films directly to foreign audiences. Undoubtedly the same
dilemmas regarding objectives and content will be faced in
this new medium. When the novelty wears off, it will be the
message and not the medium that will prevail. Material designed to appeal to what an American audience believes
should be broadcast abroad will be likely to suffer the same
fate as older material similarly fashioned.

Books and films pose some of the same problems. The
credible USIS library overseas will contain well-known
works of American literature as well as current works on
politics. From time to time there have been complaints from
members of Congress or special interest groups regarding the
selection of liberal works or the absence of conservative books
or vice versa. In general, however, libraries have been able to
operate under less scrutiny than the daily broadcasts of the
Voice of America.

For many years documentary films were an important
staple of any USIS program overseas. The videotape is gradu-
ally replacing the 16mm film. In either case, the inventories
tend to be favorable films, many of them made especially for
USIS.

To many of us who managed USIS programs overseas, the
exchange of persons program is the most effective part. Those
who have been educated in the United States or visited for
short periods, if they have effectively caught something of the
spirit and motivation of our society, are among our best advocates abroad. Many will return to significant positions within
a foreign government and will, in future years, provide access
and counsel to U.S. representatives.

This phase of the program has also been responsible for
sending American lecturers and cultural presentations
abroad. In general, individuals and groups have been chosen
without regard to their political views. From time to time
administrations have sought to screen selections, but this

practice, when revealed, has generally brought both public and congressional condemnation. The agency and the public have shown a tolerance for divergent views within limits; this part of the program has gained credibility as a result.

In areas where the U.S. political message is resisted, the exchange program is another "good will" instrument. The United States provides, both through USIS and the academic assistance program, short-term visitors' grants. To those who devise and support the grant program in the United States, these visits are seen not only as educational efforts but also as recognition of future leaders. In many countries, they are seen by officials and their friends only as "favors" for services rendered or to be rendered. In countries where benefits of any value are traditionally bestowed only in response to a favor, benefits that do not carry reciprocal rewards are viewed with puzzlement and sometimes suspicion. Once more, the true intentions of an American program are obscured, the message blunted.

Despite the largely favorable view of the exchange of persons program both at home and abroad, neither administrations nor the Congress, except for a few special friends, have ever been generous to the program or given it a high priority. At first lodged in the State Department, it was required to compete for funds with the broader requirements of foreign affairs. Moved to USIA in 1977, it has fared little better. Only strong support in the Congress prevented the Reagan administration from cutting the program drastically, even though it was pointed out that in the critical Caribbean region nearly 4,000 students had gone to the Soviet Union on government scholarships in the previous years compared to 143 on U.S. government aid.

Again, priorities are set by domestic attitudes. The exchange program is less immediate. Substantial government assistance to foreign students encounters the belief that this is something private institutions and foundations—or the foreign governments—should do. When the study demonstrating the large flow of young people from the Caribbean to the Soviet Union was brought to the attention of some members of Congress, their response was that a much larger number were coming to the United States, but on private funding. While this may be true, the assumption must be that those coming on private funds are from wealthier segments of Caribbean society. Those going to the Soviet Union are likely to be from poorer families. The U.S. attitude of neglect toward officially subsidized educational exchange runs the risk that, in future years, U.S. influence will largely be confined to the upper strata of the economic ladder in an area on America's doorstep.

U.S. exchange programs also suffer from complex procedures. Most foreign countries, including America's Western allies, place students in universities through a central government agency. The independent academic community in the United States resists this; the U.S. government must work through private agencies and require foreign students to apply directly to American universities. These applicants must ferret out their needs in the vast supermarket of American higher education and individually contact universities and arrange financial help. For some in developing countries this is an almost impossible task. The most cultural affairs officers can do abroad is to counsel student applicants generally on U.S. procedures and point them toward appropriate institutions.

The effective exchange of students, professors, and artists over the years has been largely the result of the effort spearheaded by Senator William Fulbright to use surplus currencies available in the postwar period to support cooperative binational programs. With the exhaustion of these funds, the support now comes from congressional appropriations and matching funds from foreign governments. Selection of recipients of Fulbright grants has been a problem in some countries. Not every country abroad has been willing to let a binational commission choose those who will go abroad.

In many countries this has traditionally been the prerogative of the government; the concept of an outside voice in the selection is alien. In some cases, USIS representatives have been forced to resist efforts by foreign officials to give preference to less qualified political or family favorites.

These information and cultural affairs programs have been developed with attitudes and interests of the American public and the Congress in mind—although USIA materials cannot be distributed in the United States. To be effective, the programs and materials must be adapted to a worldwide audience with greatly diversified interests and reactions.

When USIA was organized in 1948, its message was directed largely at Europe. Europe is still important—as the question of missile deployment in 1983 demonstrated—although there are occasional arguments in the agency and in the Congress about whether it is necessary to spend USIA funds in friendly European countries. With the creation of new nations in the succeeding years the task of USIA became more complicated. There were early assumptions that the new nations would be automatically receptive to messages and overtures from the United States. U.S. policymakers soon learned the power and sensitivity of nationalism and of the solidarity of the so-called Third World nations. U.S. information program planners faced three problems in the new nations: the creation of undue expectations, the identification with unpopular local issues and local regimes, and the vulnerability to violence. Each of these has played a role in reducing the impact and effectiveness of the American message overseas.

In a largely authoritarian world, interpreters of U.S. democracy encounter enormous obstacles. American political principles and the American way of life often are seen as more threatening and more revolutionary than those of the communist world. In many countries, the message from the United States is heard and viewed differently by three audiences. The leadership want the support of the United

States. The "communism" they fear and from which they wish to be protected is represented by any domestic opposition movement, whether Soviet backed or not, that threatens their power and special privilege. The intelligentsia, often bitterly opposed to the anti-intellectual and oppressive attitudes of the ruling group, accept the American message only to the degree it appears to support their own demands for a greater voice. American policies that seem to support the authoritarian rulers will be rejected, no matter how well they are packaged. The mass of the people may watch or listen to that which is specially tailored to their culture, perhaps appreciate the effort, but find little in the basic message to which they can relate.

With all three audiences, the total message transmitted through USIA is seen in the light of the U.S. position on issues of local concern. In Arab countries, no matter how effectively the perfidy of the Soviets is painted, the message will be blunted if U.S. policy appears totally in support of Israel. Many in black Africa will look at the United States and its worldwide policies solely in terms of official U.S. attitudes toward South Africa. It is not that many countries love the Soviets more; the answer lies rather in their strong displeasure with regional U.S. policies.

In 1967, Libyans were deeply embarrassed that their forces had not gone to fight with the Egyptians and others against the Israelis. The strong popular belief was that the United States had put pressure on King Idris to prevent their involvement. For three months after the war, few Libyans would speak to an American. My only conversations as ambassador were on official matters at the Ministry of Foreign Affairs. One day I passed a Libyan official on the street who before the war had been a close friend. I greeted him and he returned the greeting. I said I would like to come and visit him in his office. "No," he whispered, "I will come to your house tomorrow evening." He came, and we sat in the garden and talked. One of the principal charges against the United

States had been that the U.S. Air Force had flown air cover for the Israelis bombing Cairo in the 1967 war. My friend said in the course of this conversation, "I know in my head that you did not support the Israelis in their attack on Cairo, but in my heart I cannot admit it. If I do so, it means that two million Jews, whom we have always considered as second class citizens, have humiliated eighty million Arabs, and I cannot live with that humiliation."

This identification of the United States with local issues has meant that, even before recent waves of terrorism, United States information establishments abroad were targets of protests and acts of violence by elements opposed to U.S. policies. In some cases, the actions may be clearly traced to communist organizations. In many more the action may be by local groups opposed to United States international policies or, frequently in Third World countries, by groups that saw the United States as a supporter of unpopular policies of their local government. The USIS offices in Baghdad, Iraq, where I served as public affairs officer, were destroyed twice by local mobs, in 1948 and 1952. On the first occasion, the ostensible reason was U.S. support for Israel. On the second, public ire against an unpopular treaty with the United Kingdom was vented on the more accessible target, the USIS.

On another occasion in Baghdad, a local newspaper ran a series of scurrilous attacks on our economic assistance program. I visited the editor and invited him to visit the project, which he had described as the construction of barracks for foreign occupying soldiers. I gave him the choice of any day he wanted. He hesitated and then said, "Look, I don't really care what you are doing there. My job as a journalist is to attack this government in power and you are supporting that government."

The awareness of strong local sensitivities on international issues makes U.S. officials naturally cautious about what is disseminated at their posts. In the Middle East, ambassadors and USIS officials have frequently excised wireless file items that are too explicit in describing U.S. support for Israel, or they have removed from libraries books that would he offensive to an Arab reader. In countries that are militantly nonaligned and wish to avoid "cold war involvement," anticommunist or anti-Soviet items have been edited or removed either at the discretion of the Embassy or by the request of local authorities. In both cases, the U.S. officials have believed that such actions were necessary if the U.S. information program as a whole was to continue.

To adapt the U.S. message to local circumstances in the interests of security and acceptability inevitably masks the true content of American policy. The USIS program becomes more of a public relations activity than the hard-hitting counterpropaganda effort that many at home desire. Books are seen not as tools with a message but as gifts to use on visits to local authorities or responses to other favors. Films, chosen for the absence of offensive foreign policy messages, are used for entertainment at representational affairs. Access to libraries becomes a privilege accorded to those friendly to the Embassy.

Sometime in 1942, Loy Henderson, then U.S. minister in Iraq, visited an Islamic cultural society in Nejef, a Shia holy city in Iraq. He promised them a set of the *Encyclopaedia Britannica*, but since it was wartime he was never able to obtain one. Ten years later, when I was public affairs officer in Iraq, he wrote asking me to buy a set from my USIS program funds and present it to this organization. After some effort, the appropriate organization in Nejef was located. On the appointed day I was ushered into the presence of several Shia religious leaders. The room was a dimly lit reception hall in an annex to an old mosque. A dust-covered bookcase stood against the wall. I could make out other impressive volumes in several languages behind lock and key. With suitable references to Ambassador Henderson and his visit, I presented the box of volumes, representing $180 out of my program budget. I am certain that these books joined the others behind the dusty glass door. I have often wondered whether anyone ever thereafter referred to them. As the fundamentalist Islamic movement spread through the Middle East, did even one among the Shiah mullahs ever think back and say to himself, "I view the United States favorably. The American Minister once presented us with the *Encyclopaedia Britannica*"? I doubt it.

Inevitably the USIA programs raised expectations, particularly in developing countries. Daily circulation of material designed to trumpet the accomplishments and determination of the United States as evidence of superiority over the communist world creates unrealistic expectations. The U.S. emphasis on freedom and democracy falls on the ears of those that expect the United States to help them achieve a greater measure of local freedom. Items that herald new technical or scientific developments bring requests for help in obtaining the hardware—help U.S. embassies can seldom give. Many of the often bitter anti-American expressions I have encountered as a representative abroad can be traced to the disappointment or disillusionment of those who take our information and our messages at face value—as applying to them.

Each year as budget time approaches, officers of USIS in the field are asked for evidence of the effectiveness of the programs. Anecdotes and statistics flow into Washington and are eagerly scanned by those seeking to justify the total program or their particular part. A quote from a foreign official that he or she listened to the Voice of America and was impressed by the commentary is seized on like a jewel. Because there is so often little else, supporters fall back on statistics regarding the correspondence received or the use of libraries or the number of column inches of USIS releases used in local newspapers. But the reaction of those sitting daily in a library or reading a story on U.S. agriculture in an Indonesian newspaper is not measured. Statistics do not demonstrate that the basic objective of USIS to lead foreign minds to support U.S. policies is achieved.

Official information programs are nevertheless important to the United States in many ways. They provide a rapid means of disseminating information on U.S. policies. They supply throughout the world materials for those who want to know more about the United States. Educational exchange programs, as limited as they are, offer to students and teachers American alternatives. But, although the programs may be effective in conveying honest images of the United States, they may well not be persuasive in overcoming the many obstacles to the full acceptance and support of U.S. foreign policies.

While inherent weaknesses and contradictions exist within the program itself, the greatest challenge comes not from abroad, but from the parallel private media that give to the rest of the world contrasting pictures of the United States, its motives, and its methods.

The U.S. diplomat abroad, in most countries, works amid a flood of information about America. The official agency of the United States and the image it tries to project run directly into the competition of other versions of policy and other images disseminated through the private media. Newspapers such as the Paris edition of the *International Herald Tribune* and the *Asian Wall Street Journal* are widely read by elites around the world. Supplemented by the major news magazines that print editions in several corners of the world, these organs present the same varied views on policy and diverse pictures of life in the United States that readers receive at home. Even in the Soviet Union, a special file of items from the Western press is circulated to high officials. It is naive to think that official views can be presented that ignore the many other versions in the worldwide U.S. media.

American newspapers and journals are supplemented by films and by the growing circulation of commercial videocassettes and television programs rebroadcast in foreign countries. The most popular are often those that are the most sensational—and the most violent. It is small wonder that the image of the United States as a land of ostentatious wealth, cowboys, Indians, and gangsters is hard to suppress. As an ambassador, supporting the principle of the free flow of information, I have on occasion been instructed to intervene with a foreign government to prevent restrictions on the circulation of U.S. films; I was not always convinced that it was in the broader interest of the reputation of our nation to do so.

Americans tend to regard the widespread circulation of their films, books, TV serials, and consumer goods as a positive element. I have been asked, "How do you explain the fact that, even among those who perpetrate terrorist acts against us, things American seem to be popular?" Not atypical was the story told me by a newspaper reporter who interviewed a particularly anti-American leader in another country. On the way out, the leader's bodyguard asked the reporter how he could get a visa for the United States.

There are occasionally circumstances in which a presentation abroad of U.S. life and politics is literally incomprehensible. I recall showing the film *All the President's Men* (about the Watergate scandal) to a group of Asian officials. They could not understand what the president had done wrong.

Entertainment exports from the United States that build dreams of an exciting land of wealth, glamour, and action do little to correct the negative political images; they may even reinforce it. The often violent and explicit films, books, and magazines are sought after because they are "forbidden fruit" in a traditional society. Americans are seen as corrupting the youth by those who seek to maintain and strengthen traditional social and religious patterns. And the youths who undertake the acts of violence against Americans probably relax by watching an American film of crime and sex.

Because of the pictures and the words broadcast through private channels, our official messages, to be credible, must present enough of the flaws and problems of American society to be consistent with what is flowing through the private media. If they do, however, they dilute the full impact of the more positive image they seek to project and create. It is, in fact, difficult to determine whether the image of diversity and conflict that is projected abroad by the American media does us harm. Clearly it provides a basis for adversaries to propagate their own image of the United States. But perhaps the audiences around the world are, after all, sophisticated and able to distinguish entertainment from fact. If that is so, then a balanced and credible official information program has a chance to be effective.

XV

✒

THE AMERICAN CITIZEN

AMERICAN CITIZENS overseas like to see the flag flying over an embassy or consulate. They want to touch a bit of American soil. But, having entered the official precincts, they are not always certain just why they are there or what all those diplomats inside are doing. Americans live uneasily with government, whether their own or someone else's, whether at home or abroad.

Officials are at best tolerated; on occasion they are resented. And diplomats are, after all, officials. At the same time, no part of the U.S. diplomats' responsibilities has a higher priority than the welfare of the private citizen. This priority is generated by the basic American concern for the individual and reinforced by strong congressional interest. Paradoxically for a nation with so strong a private enterprise tradition, the U.S. diplomats' responsibilities toward the private American business people and their enterprises abroad are much less clearly defined.

The task of responding to the needs of individual citizens overseas is in the hands of consuls—when they are not issuing visas to foreign tourists and immigrants. But the visa func-

198

tion is important, too. In administering the U.S. immigration laws overseas, the diplomat is the gatekeeper to the United States. In the early 1950s, I was a consul in Norway, assisting in the issuance of visas under a special section of the immigration act for persons displaced by World War II. Young Poles who had been taken by the Germans to work in mines in northern Norway and Finland could enter the United States if they could find relatives already in America. To those young men, the issuance of a visa to the United States seemed the last chance to escape from the dark future of war-torn Europe. The tragedy of those who could not establish their eligibility was balanced with the ecstatic joy demonstrated by those admitted. Even now, in the late 1980s, the United States represents to hundreds of thousands in Eastern Europe their last best hope for the future. The American consul is the door to that hope.

In the function of protecting U.S. citizens, the consul is a combination of parish priest and city clerk, helping to get fellow citizens out of jail, issuing replacement passports, settling citizenship problems, handling the effects of the deceased, seeking to reunite families, and registering births.

Each of these consular functions is personally, emotionally, and politically charged, and of direct interest to members of the U.S. Congress.

Treatises on diplomacy seldom address this aspect of the diplomat's job, concentrating on the broader and seemingly more dramatic foreign policy issues. Yet the proper resolution of cases involving U.S. citizens demands the same type of access, often at the highest levels, the same delicacy of approach, and the same careful husbanding of the time of officials as do other issues. Even that which may seem, on the surface, trivial can require extraordinary efforts, particularly if the case is one that has been brought to the attention of the Congress or the press.

During my career, I have spent many hours in working with foreign police on such cases as the disappearance of an

American radio reporter and on repatriating an American accused of passport fraud. As an ambassador I once had to arrange with a minister of justice for the release from jail of three midwestern schoolteachers arrested for nude bathing on a beach.

Citizens are frequently surprised to find that they are under the jurisdiction of local law when abroad. They want not only to be free of the orders of their own government, but of the local government as well. U.S. diplomats have had to explain to Americans caught in the shackles of local law that they, as visitors, are under the jurisdiction of that law. U.S. diplomats can recommend lawyers, observe their trials, and, if the government is friendly, perhaps negotiate an early release from a sentence.

Our ambassador to Saudi Arabia some years ago engaged in a protracted negotiation with that government to obtain the release of an oil company employee who had been arrested for a traffic violation. Only by seeing the king and suggesting a Christmas amnesty was the ambassador able to obtain the release. More recently, in Turkey, in Mexico, and in many other capitals, U.S. diplomats have expended major efforts—not always successfully—to obtain the release of Americans arrested on narcotics charges. If not resolved, such cases can become serious irritants in relations between governments. Public charges in the United States against a foreign government because of actual or perceived affronts to American citizens can spark strong negative reactions in the other country.

At the same time, the authority of U.S. diplomats over American citizens abroad is surprisingly limited. As the Jonestown mass suicide in Guyana in 1978 illustrated, the United States has no authority to intervene, even when there is the suspicion of bizarre and criminal acts. That remains an issue for the local government.

The U.S. diplomatic concern over the U.S. citizen extends to those citizens and their relatives caught up in the restrictive emigration policies of other countries, particularly in Eastern Europe. In that region, cases involving divided families occupy a major place on the diplomatic agenda. Such cases arise either when an American citizen has married someone in an Eastern European country and seeks the emigration of the spouse or when an Eastern government refuses to permit the emigration of one member of a family bound for the United States. While I was under secretary, I made a special trip to Poland in the interest of more than a hundred family reunification cases; one congressional office told me they had received more than 1,700 pieces of mail in one month on family reunification issues.

This national concern over the individual citizen extends to communities of U.S. nationals caught in situations of war or danger. The responsibility of the ambassador and staff in such situations involves not only the safety of the individuals but also delicate diplomatic negotiations with a foreign government in times of crises. The anticipation of possible trouble in a country or region leads most U.S. ambassadors to establish some form of regular communication with the American community. In sharing information, the diplomat must avoid being alarmist while giving the community the confidence that the embassy is on top of a potentially troubling situation. In well over a hundred instances since World War II, U.S. embassies have had to recommend and arrange the evacuation of American citizens from trouble spots. The United States is often the first country to order such action. An embassy recommendation to the American community in a foreign country that conditions have deteriorated to the point where the safety of U.S. citizens can no longer be assured, however, has profound implications. It can generate concern if not panic among the local population and other foreign nationals. At a time when the United States must count on the cooperation of the local government, such a statement can create serious difficulties with that government. The decision is made, generally, by the ambassador in consultation with Washington, if time permits. No such decision is made capriciously.

When conditions permit, the community is usually evacuated in phases. A U.S. embassy abroad has no authority to force non-official citizens to leave a country or a region, and in some cases citizens refuse to go. Embassies have standby plans for moving a community and for a "safe haven." But the mission can only recommend departure. The first recommendation usually applies to dependent spouses and children. The next phase will urge the departure of nonessential personnel.

In countries where there are other communities of citizens of friendly and allied countries, the U.S. embassy is willing to coordinate planning and recommendations for evacuation with such embassies, but frequently finds that other countries are more reluctant to reach the decision to move out their citizens than is the United States. American diplomats are conscious that harm to U.S. citizens through failure to recommend timely departure appears to be a more serious matter in Washington than it is in any other capital. Whenever there is a disaster abroad, Congress and the press want to know immediately what Americans were on the spot and what has happened to them. This concentration on the safety of Americans can rile foreign sensitivities. The U.S. ambassador to Mexico at the time of the serious earthquake in Mexico City in 1985, appearing to ignore the sufferings of the Mexicans, was quoted as saying, "We have been extremely fortunate as a nation" because more Americans had not been injured or killed.

Although the responsibility of protecting individual Americans and American communities overseas has created problems, on the whole the history is one of cooperation. Foreign governments have either understood the concerns in Washington at critical moments or have seen the virtues of removing from their responsibility a sizeable group of American citizens. The role of the diplomat in protecting U.S. citizens has been reasonably well defined in Washington and accepted abroad.

The responsibility of U.S. diplomats toward the individual business representative and corporate entities abroad is much less well defined. Business attitudes toward official representatives abroad are reflections of the complex relationship between business and government in the United States.

For many decades, U.S. businesses conducted their own foreign relations abroad, dealing directly with local governments. This was particularly true in Latin America and, in the early days of oil development, in the Persian Gulf states and Saudi Arabia. The expansion of official U.S. representation abroad, the growing role of local governments, particularly after decolonization, and the internationalization of many business and trade issues brought the U.S. government more into business negotiations. This greater role of official representatives was not universally welcomed. Business is motivated by profit; the responsibility of its overseas managers is to a distant Board of Directors. In the face of tough foreign competition, the business representative wants as little interference as possible from any government, including his own. What American business wants is a U.S. policy that will help American companies make sales and obtain contracts in a period of growing competition with other major trading nations. The conventional wisdom within much of the business community abroad has been that the American embassy will do little to help; an extreme form was once expressed to me by an American businessman: "When I want help around here, I go to the British embassy."

There is no doubt that European governments and the Japanese will make representations to foreign governments on behalf of their own individual companies in a way that U.S. diplomats cannot. Their trade administrations are prepared, when an award of a major foreign government contract is at stake, to choose one company or group of companies and then, through strong diplomatic efforts, to push that bid. While the general effort on behalf of U.S. business has been strengthened in recent years through the organization of a foreign commercial service, neither the United States government nor American business has ever wanted to adopt the "chosen instrument" approach.

I once ran into trouble seeking to assist one company. In Libya in the mid-1960s, Boeing and the British Aircraft Corporation were competing to sell a new generation of planes to the Libyan national airline. Because Boeing was the only U.S. firm in the field, I felt I could, as ambassador, properly speak to Libyan officials on behalf of that bid. A telegram to Washington mentioned my efforts on behalf of Boeing. I was reprimanded and told that I would have to arrange for all other U.S. manufacturers of similar aircraft to enter the field and that I was to make general, rather than particular, representations to the government on behalf of the excellence of U.S. aircraft. That obviously was a less compelling approach than that being made by my British colleague on behalf of a single firm. Despite the complications posed by Washington, Boeing won the contract.

The official U.S. promotion and protection of firms overseas with American stockholders has become further complicated by the internationalization of business. Ownership of large corporations is now often spread among stockholders of many nationalities. A U.S. company may work through foreign-owned subsidiaries. For reasons of economy and under demands from foreign governments for "indigenization," more and more U.S. companies are turning to nationals of the country to staff senior positions overseas.

The presence of foreign nationals and, in particular, of nationals of the host country in positions of major responsibility for U.S.-owned firms raises issues of consultation. Good reasons exist for frequent consultation between embassy representatives and U.S. company officials overseas on matters of community morale, security, education, and developments affecting the economic climate. Nationals of the host country are sometimes placed in a difficult position if they are expected to comment and to act as U.S. nationals; quite naturally, they feel an obligation to keep their own government informed of major attitudes and developments in the business world—and of discussions with foreign governments.

Beyond the question of the responsibility of a U.S. embassy for the commercial promotion of American products is that of the appropriate role when companies with American equity are involved in problems with foreign governments. This is an area of diplomatic involvement that has never been fully defined in the United States. The U.S. government is not officially a party to a dispute between private U.S. companies and a foreign government. Congressional legislation requires that U.S. officials abroad assist companies faced with nationalization or expropriation, but beyond this the ambassador has few standing instructions. Two examples will illustrate the anomalous nature of the ambassador's role.

I was ambassador to Libya during the years of rapid oil development in that country. The Libyan government of King Idris at that time wanted to avoid the dependence on a single oil company or group of oil companies that had been the pattern in the Persian Gulf. To accomplish this, the country was divided into numerous smaller concession areas and offered to many companies, the well-known major companies as well as independent companies, many new to foreign exploration. In 1966, a serious dispute developed between these two groups of American companies over a tax formula. At a time when the unilateral imposition of contract changes by a government was still a novelty, the Libyan government threatened to legislate a change favored by the major companies. The U.S. government wanted to avoid this, and I was instructed to do what I could. Much of my diplomacy involved convincing the skeptical U.S. companies that my role could be useful and that neither side would benefit from a unilateral imposition of changes. Ultimately I was able to bring the lawyers for the two sides together in the embassy residence for a carefully defined negotiation and to present the Libyan government changes agreed to by the industry. Neither instruction from Washington nor a diplomatic textbook gave a formula for dealing with such a situation, yet it was one with serious implications, both for the future of the oil industry in the region and for future U.S.-Libyan relations.

In Indonesia in 1975, the Indonesian national oil company, Pertamina, overextended and accumulated more than $3 billion in debts, largely owed to syndicates of American banks.

I was advised one day that a Texas bank, part of a wider syndicate, was going to call its loan to Pertamina because of a delay in Pertamina's payment of interest and principal. I sensed that, if that were to happen, it would start a serious demand for payment and create an Indonesian-U.S. problem that would have wider repercussions. There was no time to get any instructions from Washington and little precedent for official intervention in a matter that was, basically, between private banks and a quasi-official agency of the Indonesian government.

I decided to approach the Texas bank representative and to ask him to delay his notification to Pertamina by forty-eight hours. I then went to the Indonesian government to advise them of the bank's intention to call the note. I asked whether they would back up the Pertamina debt. The Indonesian government agreed to stand behind the debt and a set of actions followed that, over time, resolved what could have been a serious financial crisis.

Even though I regarded my action as having been beneficial to all sides, I spent a certain amount of time in the ensuing weeks explaining to bankers and to people in Washington why I had intervened. Again, there was no manual of guidance to deal with problems of this kind. Given the ambiguous relationship between business and government in the United States, it is unlikely that there ever will be.

Not even senators are clear about this relationship. In

1970, the Senate Foreign Relations Committee held a series of hearings on corrupt practices overseas. One of the committee's witnesses had been an accountant for an American company operating in Libya when I was ambassador there. The accountant had given the committee counsel detailed information on payments the company had made to Libyan officials. I was also called as a witness and asked if I had been aware of these payments.

"Senator," I recall replying, "rumors were rife that companies were making payments to Libyan officials to assist them in getting concessions. When I would raise this occasionally with company officials, their reply would always be, 'We do nothing of this kind, but there are companies that do.'"

The senator then asked me, "But don't you have authority to investigate such charges?"

"No, Senator, these contracts are between a private company and a foreign government. There is no law that gives a U.S. representative the right or the obligation to investigate such charges."

Out of those hearings came the Corrupt Practices Act of 1977, creating still another point of potential difference in the points of view of the diplomat and the business representative. Although the legislation placed no responsibility upon diplomats to investigate allegations of corruption by U.S. firms, the act clearly signalled the opposition of the U.S. government to the involvement of American companies in bribery, kickbacks, and other corrupt practices.

Further, embassy officers recognize, particularly in Third World countries, the relationship between corruption and internal instability. Wherever possible, U.S. diplomats seek to discourage the involvement of U.S. companies in such practices. The American commercial agent abroad, however, faces daily in many countries the demands for extra, often illegal, payments and is seldom either candid with the diplomats or sympathetic to their attitude in such matters.

Despite the many points of potential friction between the

business and diplomatic worlds, efforts have increased in recent years to establish better means of communicating. U.S. Chambers of Commerce abroad, for example, have invited diplomats to speak and to attend meetings. Individual ambassadors have made efforts to establish close ties with business communities. But no amount of effort will ever totally eliminate a basic divergence of views and attitudes that is basic to American society.

XVI

✒

DIPLOMACY AND
AMERICAN DEMOCRACY

THIS BOOK HAS BEEN about diplomacy, and primarily about how the United States of America conducts its affairs with other nations. The conclusions are not comforting. The United States fails to listen, or ignores much of what the world is thinking and feeling. While still respected for their ideals, Americans exaggerate both their power and their influence. The Soviet Union, with its brutal system, has a better image than the reality deserves. Even in democratic nations, many say there is little to choose between the superpowers. In some traditional societies, the United States is seen as an even more destructive force than the Soviet Union.

U.S. national interests have suffered from internal revolutions, particularly in the Third World. The elaborate diplomatic and intelligence networks of the nation have failed to anticipate radical political change. In many cases, the United States has been seen as the enemy; significant U.S. advantages have been lost when a ruler has been overthrown. U.S. hopes for peace in troubled areas have been dashed. The United States has at times seemed more a part of the problem than of the solution. Having lost its position of control in the

209

United Nations, the United States finds itself more often re-
viled than praised in the body it helped create. Terrorists,
products of the frustrated fringes of unresolved problems,
have made Americans targets.

In a cloud of national delusion, the United States has
failed to recognize its diplomatic successes such as Camp
David or to acknowledge its failures such as Lebanon. Successes are criticized and failures rationalized. Leaders and
policies are partly at fault, but much of the problem also lies
in the nature of American society and the way it relates to the
rest of the world.

Does all of this represent a failure for U.S. diplomacy? In
the minds of many Americans, it does. If blame is to be
assessed because the world fails to accept U.S. policies, Americans tend to blame not only the foreigner but also the diplomats who have failed to persuade others of the correctness of
the U.S. view.

The diplomat representing the free democratic structure
of the United States works under many handicaps. Foreign
policies created under the pressures of U.S. domestic political
concerns, giving short shrift to international realities, cannot
easily be "sold" to others. The confusion of voices resulting
from democratic debate threatens the credibility of official
statements. Open criticism of foreign regimes and leaders
rubs raw nerves abroad. The undisguised temptation to manipulate other societies creates suspicions abroad not easily
dispelled. The perceived failure to respond to the economic
needs of the developing world creates a constant atmosphere
of disappointment. The constitution gives the U.S. diplomat
less authority in international negotiations than a foreign
counterpart. The capricious indifference to the qualifications
for many diplomatic appointments, even in significant posts,
is a matter of amusement, if not incredulity, abroad. An infi-
nitesimal amount of the national budget is set aside for foreign affairs.

To most citizens, these are not matters of persuasive significance. Americans ask these questions: Is there not a resurgence of democracy? Does not the United States remain strong and important? Are we not still the most powerful nation in the world? Are not others looking to us for hope and security? Should not a nation base its foreign policies on domestic concerns?

The answer, today, to most of these questions is yes. The United States remains an unchallenged symbol of a free society, often envied by the very people who attack it and despise it. No country equals the United States as a mecca for those fleeing from oppression or privation. The names of America's founding fathers are still mentioned and revered by those seeking to improve their political lot. The manifest U.S. interest in the human rights of others continues to generate hope and expectations. The fact that foreign policy is based on domestic concerns is a matter of strength, not of weakness. No foreign policy of a democracy can be effective that does not ultimately have domestic support.

To many who put their store in the freedom of the individual, the United States looms as the only alternative to a world of oppression. This fact has outweighed the difficulties in the U.S. relationship with others. However skillful and uncomplicated may be the diplomacy of the Soviet Union, that nation is rarely seen as a desirable alternative to democracy.

Not long before his death, columnist Joseph Kraft wrote, following a review of the efforts of other countries to reconcile their policies with the United States, "One lesson that emerges from this record is that the rest of the world genuinely needs the United States. Interdependence makes the United States indispensable to everybody. This country can cut up rough—can make what traditional diplomats regard as egregious errors—without paying a great price."*

This immunity from normal diplomatic errors has preserved the U.S. position in the world despite the dramatic

*The *Washington Post*, October 24, 1985.

changes and complications of the last half of the twentieth century. Will they be enough beyond this era?

The problems of the U.S. diplomat are symptomatic of a deeper issue in U.S. society. Americans continue to resist the responsibilities of a great power. They dream of quick, dramatic, and heroic actions and see these as a solution to long-term, highly complex challenges.

When foreign policy achievements were reached in the last half of the century, they took place because presidents and administrations were prepared to defy a prevailing national sentiment. Virtually every one of the major diplomatic landmarks seen by the rest of the democratic world as praiseworthy accomplishments have been carried out against a strong measure of American indifference or resistance. These include the entry into World War II, the North Atlantic, ABM, and Panama Canal treaties, and the SALT agreements. As the Reagan years have demonstrated, presidents are more popular who appeal to the basically chauvinistic and assertive tendencies of the American people; they are more popular, but they accomplish less in the field of foreign relations.

What concerns the U.S. diplomat, looking beyond U.S. borders, is whether the United States can continue to afford the luxury of relative indifference to foreign relations and casual capriciousness toward diplomacy in a world increasingly threatening to the Americans' way of life and interests.

An additional paragraph from Joseph Kraft's column quoted above is pertinent:

"But it remains hard to believe that stiff-arming can work forever. The United States has an interest in reaching agreements on many thorny issues. To get accords, it makes sense to pay out a little bit of the diplomatic capital that has been built up over the past four years. For there applies to diplomatic capital a rule that applies to other kinds of capital: you can't take it with you."

The strength of the United States continues to be based to

a considerable extent on the expectations that others have of us. A frequent response by foreigners, defending their criticisms of the United States, is, "We expect more of you." Despite failures, Europeans and friends in Asia still believe that the United States would be prepared to assist them if their countries were genuinely threatened by the Soviet Union. The belief in the power of the United States to mobilize for a major threat persists and is a major element in the strength of the U.S. global position. The United States frightens its allies and friends by its occasional bellicosity and unpredictability, but the expectation of support remains. Is this expectation justified?

The conservative tide that swept the United States in the 1980s believes that the greater assertiveness of the United States has improved its position in the world. Less attention to some of the peripheral sensitivities and more to fundamental U.S. national interests, in their view, have improved the standing of America. The relative absence of strong reaction in many areas to this assertiveness has been seen as proof that the world wants the United States to be strong and to use its strength.

The conservative approach is based on an assumption that the position of the United States of the 1950s can be reestablished, a position of such strength that the United States could act as it wished without regard for world opinion. That was not true then; it is unlikely to be true today.

The battle between East and West for influence occurs not so much in those countries we call our "firm friends" as in those weaker areas where feelings on such issues as the Arab-Israeli conflict and apartheid run deep. A case can be made that these regions of the world have been relatively silent in reacting to locally unpopular U.S. policy not through acquiescence or enthusiasm, but through a feeling that the United States is no longer a just arbiter of regional problems. Such a mood can only produce pressures for national policies in other countries independent of the involvement and interests

of the United States. The irony would be that a more assertive, conservative policy, designed to make the United States
stronger globally, would have the opposite effect.

Sir Harold Nicolson, in his work on *Diplomacy*, saw the
world moving from a balance of largely European powers to a
bipolar world in which the United States and the Soviet
Union were the major players. The new diplomacy of the
immediate postwar period pitted an untidy democratic diplomacy against the calculated and unscrupulous diplomacy of
the Soviet Union. Nicolson raised doubts whether democratic
diplomacy would succeed.

Democratic diplomacy, at least as practiced in the United
States, has suffered from the conflicting currents of open
policy making and a lack of respect and of confidence on the
part of U.S. political circles. Such diplomacy, however, has
not been the loser in the contest with the Soviet Union. The
recognition by a large part of the world of the importance of
the United States in the achievement and maintenance of a
global balance has overcome any possible weakness of democratic diplomacy. The United States is successful more for
what it is than for what it does.

The position of the United States and the West in general
has benefitted for the last four decades from certain stabiliz-
ing forces. For most of this period, leadership was still in the
hands of men and women of a generation that remembered
World War II and experienced the tragedies of underestimating the challenge to democratic values. The leaders of the
newly independent states, while often radical and anti-West-
ern, were still products of a European-dominated system.
Their education and their personal friendships led them to
maintain links with the Western democracies. The Soviet
Union has represented a major threat, but has not been totally irresponsible or dangerously adventurous in its challenges to the West. The United Nations, however imperfectly,
provided a place for the airing of grievances and the discussion of problems. The world still played by certain under-

stood rules benefitting the West; major conflict was inhibited by the nuclear balance.

In such circumstances, the threats to the United States and its allies were manageable. "Politics as usual," with its concentration on domestic concerns to the exclusion of serious regard for how others felt, was still a feasible luxury for the United States. A casual and capricious approach to diplomacy did not pose serious risks. In the last decade of the twentieth century, that relatively satisfactory situation may be changing. New generations are emerging into leadership positions in Europe, Asia, and the Third World that do not have the links of memory or inherent sympathy with the United States. The strong U.S. role in saving Western Europe is now learned only from history books.

At this writing, some of the emerging new leaders are themselves conservative and share the values and concerns of the United States. But will this last under their temptations of new ties with Eastern Europe, fears of conflict, and the pressures for economic nationalism in Western Europe and Japan?

Old issues involving finance, debt, and trade remain, complicated by the erosion of international agreements, such as the General Agreement on Tariffs and Trade and the Breton Woods accords, hammered out in the immediate postwar period. Already one can see the growing threat of trade wars among major Western powers. A bitter environment of competition would spill over into the weaker economies of Third World nations with disastrous consequences.

Rapid advances in science and technology create instruments that threaten traditional sovereignty. Computerized data can be sent across national lines in ways that make both control and access difficult. The exploitation of space requires the cooperation of many governments if it is to be fair, economical, and effective. New discoveries in biotechnology have implications for the entire human race that cannot be easily confined by national boundaries. The awesome possibilities of the power of the atom still require an international regime that nations have yet to establish.

During the latter half of the century, the world still respected the nation-state, even though many such states perpetuated the artificial divisions of ethnic groups created in the colonial period. The seeds existed in these artificial boundaries for bitter internal conflicts—beyond the ability of others to control or resolve. World stability was maintained, in part, because major states still had influence. Their financial power could avert the worst of economic disasters; their political power could contain, if not prevent, wars.

As debts rise, as the interest of the developed countries in former colonial territories flags, as the leaders of these newer nations find less and less in common with Europe, as new, radical social and religious movements spread through these regions, will the influence and power of the Western nations, including the United States, continue to be relevant? Already, at this writing, one can see a decline in the degree to which youths in the Middle East and Southern Africa continue to pay any attention to the ideas and thoughts of the United States and Europe.

Into the struggles in the Middle East has been injected a revitalized Islam. The turn to a militant religious tradition has affected the political stability of nearly every major Moslem state. Is this a portent for the future?

Many of the countries today considered friendly to the West have within them the seeds of change: Egypt, Mexico, Pakistan, Korea. The future course of China is uncertain. The Middle East remains a dangerous enigma. The countries of Eastern Europe will continue to search for ways to lessen the Soviet yoke.

The United States and Europe have already seen in the rise of terrorism in the 1980s the potential threat of youth nurtured in the hopeless frustrations of unresolved conflict. Could the breakup of Lebanon into fiefdoms of warring factions be a pattern that might be followed in other areas threatened by bitter factional conflict? What is the future of a South Africa where the past fabric is disintegrating into a complex of white-black, white-white, and black-black struggles?

The enthusiasm for multilateral solutions to problems, embodied in the United Nations, has declined. The United States has been among the first to turn its back not only on the international organization and its affiliated bodies, but also on such major multilateral negotiations as that on the Law of the Sea. The risk is that the only existing framework for international cooperation, however fragile, is being undermined.

In a world that may see movements growing beyond the reach of traditional national institutions, created out of the bitterness of nihilistic youth, and threats to the human condition beyond national boundaries, new approaches to international relations may be necessary. The struggle between the Soviet Union and the West may become less central as both camps look over their shoulders at circumstances outside their experience.

The United States has successfully maintained its position in the world without paying major attention to what others were saying or caring. As a Kenyan writer has said, "Americans have had their hearing aid turned off."* The hearing aid has indeed been turned off—not only to what others were saying, but to much of what U.S. diplomats have been saying as well. New potential trends of change, terrorism, disintegration, and violence no longer allow that luxury.

Despite a casual if not occasionally hostile national attitude toward diplomacy, the representatives of the United States have established access and respect around the world. They have learned difficult languages and have become experts in newly important regions. They have negotiated diffi-

---

*Ali Mazrui, in Sanford J. Ungar, ed., *Estrangement: America and the World* (Oxford University Press, 1985), pp. 179-192.

cult agreements in the national interest. They have explained and defended policies and rounded off the rough edges of unpopular U.S. actions. But diplomacy cannot be totally separated from the attitudes and priorities of a nation. The reports of the most astute observer of a foreign scene are of little value if unread or discounted.

U.S. diplomats must live with democracy's anomalies, explain them, and enthusiastically defend them. The process can work; it has in the past. Diplomacy in American democracy will continue to be vulnerable to different voices, to the competition for credibility with a free press and legislature, and to the inefficient consultation on policies with fellow democracies. To recommend that these aspects be changed is to recommend the destruction of democracy.

If change is required, it must be in the attitude toward other nations and their interests on the part of the American people and leaders. In a world that may be increasingly chaotic and threatening, democratic leaders cannot afford illusions of influence where influence does not exist; they cannot afford the search for more comforting assessments when confronted with unpleasant news. The luxury of ideology, whether from the left or the right, cannot be permitted to drive out an objective, professional approach to the conduct of relations with other countries. The issues are too serious.

The world is not prepared to tolerate indefinitely an insensitive and overbearing United States just because of what the country may represent. The result will be less American influence on critical international issues, greater hostility for the United States abroad, and less security for the nation.

Confronted with the prospect of serious reverses abroad, Americans like to suggest internal reorganizations of the policy process or a more strident information effort. These are not answers. The answer lies in policies that can be coherently explained and credibly defended. Diplomacy can then add the needed skills of implementation in the knowledge of other cultures, the skill of negotiation, the art of persuasion, and the power to observe and report.

Diplomacy is neither a capricious luxury nor an outmoded anachronism; it is and must remain vital to the security of the nation. In a world growing ever more complex, the warnings, the skills, and the advice of the diplomat are an indispensable insurance against disaster.

American diplomats must continue to listen to other societies, to sense the differences and the similarities. In so doing they can do what many Americans have so often done: convey an interest in another people, another culture, without losing the perspective of the outsider.

More and more in the future, as the world occasionally erupts and fragments, the diplomat will need a balanced sense of those eruptions, the interests of the American nation involved, and the opportunities that may exist to contribute to peace. Diplomatic adversaries will be tough, aggressive, devious, and resolute. The American diplomats will require even more patience and a stronger sense of perspective. Americans have, in the past, effectively demonstrated both.

Although major conflict has been avoided, the world today is far from friendly. The United States must pursue its interests in an arena of both friends and adversaries, but with the knowledge that it still remains for the greater part of the world's peoples a symbol of hope and freedom. Leadership in Washington can create the policies that will give meaning to national objectives, but the implementation of those policies will depend upon the skills of men and women prepared to accept the responsibilities and the risks and to pursue the art of diplomacy.

Index

221